Blessed Assurance:

The Life and Hymns of Fanny J. Crosby
John Loveland

BROADMAN PRESS

Nashville, Tennessee

4272-20
ISBN: 0-8054-7220-7

Dedication

*To Mildred, Wendell, Paula,
Karen, Joy, and Alan, who without
complaining allowed me to use time
in this work that otherwise would
have been shared with them.*

Dewey Decimal Classification: B
Subject heading: CROSBY, FANNY J.//HYMNS

Library of Congress Catalog Card Number: 77-78622
Printed in the United States of America

Foreword

For more than a hundred years, Christians around the world have been singing hymns penned by Fanny Crosby. It seems, however, that most people know little or nothing about her life.

Research for this book has stretched over five years and during these years I have come to admire this Christian lady to an extent that in the beginning I never thought possible. It seems almost that I knew her personally, and it is my sincere desire that even before you read half of these pages you will have the same feeling.

At the end of this book is a bibliography, showing the sources most used in preparing this work. Much additional help has come from people, old newspapers, letters, telephone calls, magazines, pamphlets, and books too numerous to mention. More than a hundred people have helped to make this book possible. This help has been in varying degrees, from simple words of encouragement to the furnishing of clippings and entire books. If I were asked which was the more help, the words of encouragement or the material furnished, the question would be hard to answer, for it would have been difficult indeed to complete the book without both.

Other books, some of them more than 125 years old, have been located by bookfinders, after long and painstaking searches. These also are listed in the bibliography. The newspapers and some of the magazines from which the clippings came are not listed, for in some instances the name or the date of issue is not known. Because of the large number of general reference books consulted, they are not shown.

Large volumes of material have been supplied by individuals, the Library of Congress, the New York Public Library, the Bridgeport Public Library, and The New York Institute for the Education of the Blind. In addition, photocopies have been made from stories on the subject in magazines published near the turn of the century. Some of these were found in the Saint Louis Public Library.

The Library of Congress, the New York Public Library, Metropolitan Life, and Sybil Baker furnished photographs.

As for the people who have furnished information and encouragement, it is impossible to name them all. Three ladies knew Fanny Crosby personally. Two of the ladies are related to her. Another is related to the people who bought the Fanny Crosby home. Still another is a direct descendant of William H. Doane, who wrote music for some of Fanny's hymns. Others are people who simply loved the blind writer and the hymns she wrote. A few are mentioned in the book, but because it would be difficult to draw a line and list those who helped the most, no attempt will be made to name any of them here. But may God bless them all!

As far as is practical I have written this story in chronological order, but because of the nature of some of the subject matter it is not entirely in that order.

To make the story as personal as possible—between Fanny Crosby and the reader—I have quoted liberally and verbatim from Fanny's own words. These quotations include incidents about her life, as well as her poems and hymns. All hymns and poems quoted are by Fanny Crosby, unless otherwise noted.

In quoting narrative, dialogue, poems, and hymns by Fanny Crosby, I have used material known to be public domain, either by its early copyright date or by reports furnished by the Library of Congress upon investigating the material.

Fanny Crosby was vague in writing about certain areas of her life. Research has added but little to some of these areas, but I have not padded the story with guesses. There is little supposition, and it is indicated as such by the context of my writing.

Many of the books listed in the bibliography are now a part of my personal library. It took almost five years to acquire a copy of Fanny's *The Blind Girl and Other Poems*, published in 1844, and nearly four years to get *Monterey and Other Poems*, published in 1851. I believe with one exception I have all the books that Fanny wrote, including an autographed copy of her *Bells at Evening and Other Verses*, 1897. I have an original issue of William B. Bradbury's *Golden Censer*, the hymnal containing Fanny Crosby's very first hymn, in 1864.

More recently I received a family scrapbook, including a letter by Fanny Crosby, one by a sister, and another by a niece. Besides these handwritten letters, there are detailed family records. Personal letters normally are not intended for publication and wishing to respect this privacy, I have not quoted from this scrapbook. But much information gleaned elsewhere and used in this book can be verified by these records and letters. Personal letters I have used were among those Fanny shared with the public near the turn of the century and are not from this particular collection.

I have included the human side of Fanny Crosby, her weaknesses as well as her admirable traits. Lest there be those who think I have dwelled too much on the latter and have attempted to idolize her, let me say I have not intended it so.

For the most part, her life was yielded to the Savior, allowing the Holy Spirit to work through her. So if this story exalts Jesus Christ, as I believe her life did, this effort has not been in vain. And Fanny Crosby would not have wanted it any other way.

JOHN LOVELAND

Contents

Contents

(Continued)

1
Fanny Crosby's Life Story

An arm of the Croton River carved a valley in Putnam County, New York. In that valley lay a peaceful settlement called Southeast, and at the edge of that settlement stood a modest frame house in which Frances Jane Crosby was born on March 24, 1820. Southeast is still there, although it has changed and grown. The little cottage is still there on Foggintown Road, too, and it looks very much as it did more than a hundred and fifty years ago.

The arm of the river that the Crosbys knew so well was little more than a babbling brook. It ran just a few hundred feet from their cottage, making music and speaking a language that little Fanny Crosby soon would understand.

Fanny's father was John Crosby, although she never knew much about him for he died before she was a year old. Her mother was Mercy Crosby, whose maiden name was also Crosby, and Fanny later traced this family line back to Simon and Ann Crosby, who came to Boston in 1635. Simon was one of the founders of Harvard College, and his son Thomas graduated from that institution in 1653.

A number of Fanny Crosby's ancestors were heroes in the Revolutionary War, especially in the battle at Bunker Hill. When General Warren was killed in that battle it was a Crosby, according to Fanny's information, who caught up the flag as it fell from the general's hands. Enoch Crosby, a cousin to Fanny's grandfather, was an important spy in that war and although James Fenimore Cooper never admitted it, it was widely believed that Enoch Crosby was the inspiration for Mr. Cooper's first successful novel, *The Spy*.

When Fanny was six weeks old, her eyes became inflamed and when the condition failed to clear up, the concerned parents sent for a doctor. Since the family doctor was not available, another one came and applied hot poultices to the baby's eyes. Notwithstanding the doctor's good intentions, the treatment apparently was a mistake because Fanny Crosby was blinded for life.

When John Crosby died, it was necessary for Mercy to go to work to provide for the family. Because of her work she could not spend as much time with her blind child as she wanted to, but Fanny's grandmother eagerly assisted. It was Fanny's grandmother who provided much of the girl's early training.

Fanny and her grandmother often strolled through the meadows and woods, breathing the fragrance of new mown hay and listening to the singing of the meandering brook. Fanny learned early to identify the birds by the sounds they made. And she could identify the flowers by touching their petals and smelling their sweet scent. One afternoon when a summer shower had ended, the two climbed to the crest of a hill overlooking the Croton River. Fanny breathed the fresh, clean air and listened attentively to her grandmother describe the arch and colors of a rainbow spanning the valley. The child had never seen one, nor would she ever, but it seemed that she could almost see and reach out and touch this one. And Fanny enjoyed the story her grandmother told of the first rainbow and the promise that came with it, as is recorded in the Bible!

Fanny learned to do household chores and to knit and sew, as did most girls in those days. She learned to play many of the games and sports that her sighted friends played, and she climbed the tallest trees and rode horseback so well that one would hardly know she was blind.

In the evenings, when Fanny was yet a toddler, her grandmother would pull her rocking chair near a window and have the child climb up on her lap. Together they saw the glittering stars and the crescent moon that curtained the night and they talked about faraway places. They listened to the chirping of the crickets and heard an occasional cry of a whippoorwill coming from the meadow or the wooded area not far away. They sang together the hymns that they loved so well, and at an early age Fanny wondered if she might one day write a hymn just as pretty as those they sang.

The grandmother read from the Scriptures and talked with Fanny about the heavenly Father's love, and how he had a plan for the life of every little boy and girl. The close relationship of Fanny and her grandmother must have been a part of God's plan for Fanny's life, for the memories were fond and permanent. The Scriptures she learned placed her in good stead for the work that lay ahead.

So vividly did those early memories remain with Fanny Crosby that later in life she wrote a poem to describe them:

Grandma's Rocking Chair

I am thinking of a cottage,
In a quiet, rural dell,
And a brook that ran beside it,
That I used to love so well;
I have sat for hours and listened,
While it rippled at my feet,
And I thought no other music
In the world was half so sweet.

There are forms that flit before me;
Those are times I yet recall;
But the voice of gentle Grandma
I remember best of all;
In her loving arms she held me,
And beneath her patient care
I was borne away to dreamland,
In her dear old rocking chair.

I am thinking of a promise
That I made when last we met;
'Twas a rosy summer twilight
That I never shall forget;

"Grandma's going home," she whispered,
  "And the time is drawing nigh;
Tell me, darling, will you meet her
  In our Father's house on high?"

She was looking down upon me;
  For a moment all was still;
Then I answered with emotion:
  "By the grace of God, I will."
How she clasped me to her bosom!
And we bowed our heads in prayer
Where so oft we knelt together,
  By her dear old rocking chair.

She has passed the vale of shadows,
  She has crossed the narrow sea,
And beyond the crystal river
  She is waiting now for me:
But in fancy I recall her,
  And again we kneel in prayer,
While my heart renews its promise
  By her dear old rocking chair.

2
First Trip to New York

In 1823, when Fanny Crosby was three years old, the Crosby family left Southeast and moved to North Salem, in neighboring Westchester County. Here they lived among a number of delightful Quaker families, and little Fanny was quick to learn what they called the "plain language." One old gentleman by the name of David often invited her to ride along in the farm wagon when he was going to the mill. This journey Fanny eagerly looked forward to from week to week. On some of the trips, however, when David felt he could not properly look after her, he wouldn't invite her. On these occasions, she would invite herself and crawl upon the seat beside him.

"No, thee ain't going with me," he would say.

"I tell thee I *am* going with thee to the mill," Fanny would reply.

"Well, get thy bonnet and come along," would usually be the man's final answer, and the two would soon be on their way to town with the grain.

As a small child, Fanny spent much of her time entertaining herself with some homemade toy or sometimes with one bought at the store. When she was about four years old her mother decided she was ready for a more advanced toy and called the blind child to her.

"Here, Fanny, is a *live* toy: only be careful of it and don't hurt it." She placed a tiny lamb in the girl's arms. Fanny jumped with glee and imagined herself to be Mary in a poem she had heard, about a little lamb following its mistress to school.

Fanny and the lamb became constant companions, romping through the pastures and meadows, climbing the hills, and frolicking among the birch, maple, and oak trees that grew so bountifully in the area. When they became too tired to play, Fanny sat on the ground, leaned against a giant oak, and cuddled the animal in her arms, and the two would drift off to sleep.

The lamb grew larger and less gentle. It developed the habit of butting, as sheep usually do, and often butted Fanny, sometimes knocking her down and tearing her clothing. But Fanny loved the animal nonetheless.

The lamb grew larger still and so did Fanny's bruises. Her mother became concerned for the child's safety and took the most appropriate action she knew. No one told Fanny what that action was, nor did they have to, for when she learned they were having lamb chop for dinner, she knew the fate of her pet. She grieved many days for the lamb and never developed a taste for lamb or mutton.

A successful livestock dealer and drover lived nearby. Daniel Drew later received wide publicity as a businessman and stock manipulator. Although he may not have been popular with some people because of some of his transactions, Fanny remembered him from her childhood as being the kindhearted man that had compassion for the little blind girl who had lost her only pet. He picked a choice lamb from his flock and offered it to her. The young child had no desire for another lamb, however, and politely refused it.

Fanny's grief gradually subsided and for the most part her young life was a happy one. She enjoyed the Bible and poetry her mother and grandmother read to her. She memorized much of it and at night could hear rhymes running through her head. She was glad when her mother told her some of the great poets were blind. She accepted her mother's explanation that sometimes the Lord permits one of his children to go without the sense of sight or hearing in order for the child to develop his other senses more fully. In that way a child can help carry out God's plan for his life.

She still loved her walks and her lessons in nature with her grandmother. She learned to identify the hemlock by feeling its short flat needles. Through her senses of smell and touch, she could recognize the birch, oak, maple, and spruce trees.

Fanny especially loved flowers, the way they felt and smelled. She loved the blossoms of the apple, cherry, and peach trees, and eagerly waited for the fruit she knew would follow. She happily listened to her grandmother describe the peony, pansy, sweet pea, scarlet poppy, and the red, white, and yellow roses.

Her choice stroll was the one she and her grandmother made down along the gurgling brook to gather her choice flower, the purple violet. Remembering these trips many years later, she wrote a poem called "Seeking for Violets" and one entitled "The Violet's Answer," the latter is found elsewhere in this book.

Some of Fanny's bird-friends were the redheaded woodpecker, the mockingbird, the meadowlark, the sparrow, the robin, and the goldfinch. And one she especially loved was the whippoorwill. She knew that this mottled brown bird has a large, bristled mouth and that some of the male's tail feathers were white. Although she was never to see one, she could identify it when it made its mournful sound in the middle of the night, calling its own name, "whippoorwill, whippoorwill!"

In remembrance of her feathered friends, Fanny later wrote a poem that began:

> The dewdrops are melting away, my bird,
> The sunbeams are kissing the flowers;
> And hast thou no greeting, no song of delight,
> To welcome these lovely hours?

The sixth and final verse says:

> Ah, yes, thou art happy again, my bird,
> And lonely thou ne'er shalt be;

I will make thy life like a sweet spring day,
If still thou wilt carol for me.

On March 24, 1825, Fanny celebrated her fifth birthday, and one evening a few days afterward her mother called her to her side.

"Fanny, I am going to take you on a little journey," she said. "We shall travel first in a wagon, till we come to the bank of a beautiful river, with mountains on each side of it. Then we shall get into a sailboat and sail south for many miles. After the boat ride we will be in a great city, larger than any you have ever visited. We will stay there for several days and then come home again."

The idea of making such a long trip at first thrilled Fanny. When her mother explained the purpose of the trip was for consultation with doctors regarding the possibility of surgery for her eyes, the little girl was not so joyous. It took some effort on the part of her mother to convince her that there was a chance she might be able to see. Fanny, of course, did want to see. She wished to be able to read books like other children. She wanted to enjoy the scenery about her. Finally, the anticipation of the trip outweighed the apprehension of the surgery, and Fanny agreed to go.

This was no easy decision for Fanny's mother either, for at that time there was no chloroform or ether for anesthesia. Considerable pain would necessarily be associated with such a delicate surgical procedure. But if her daughter's sight could be restored, she desperately wanted that. So plans and preparations were made.

In 1825 modes of transportation were very primitive compared to those of a few years later. Robert Fulton had built his steamboat *Clermont* only a few years before and made the successful trip up the Hudson River. Steamboats, therefore, were still few in number, and there were not yet any passenger trains, for Peter Cooper did not give locomotive *Tom Thumb* its trial run until 1830. The stagecoach was the popular means of transportation in those days. There was not even a stagecoach that ran from the rural community of North Salem to any point on the Hudson River or to New York City. The best the Crosbys could do was to take an ordinary farm wagon to the town of Sing Sing, the name was later changed to Ossinging, and a sailboat from there to their destination in New York City. And even though the entire distance was only about fifty miles, it would take the greater part of two days to get there.

On a bright April morning the Crosby family was up early. Fanny donned one of her newest dresses that looked so nice with her freshly-brushed black curls. At about eight o'clock Fanny, her mother, and a cousin climbed aboard the farm wagon and the driver urged the horses on. They made their way down the winding dirt road toward the town of Sing Sing which sprawled along the bank of the Hudson River.

They arrived at Sing Sing at 4:00 P.M., and an hour later climbed aboard the boat. The white sails took wind and the long journey southward was begun.

Before they had gone far Mrs. Crosby became ill from the motion of the boat and retired to her bunk below. Fanny and the cousin stayed on deck and the excitement sent shivers through the blind girl as she felt the boat move and heard the waves sloshing against its sides. Captain Green, who was in charge of the boat, seemed to enjoy the company of his two young passengers. He told sea stories to the children and in return for his favor, Fanny offered to sing for him. She sang "Hail Columbia, Happy Land," and when the Captain asked for another she sang "A Prisoner for Life," a verse of which says:

> Adieu, ye green fields; ye soft meadows, adieu;
> Ye hills and ye mountains, I hasten from you.
> No more shall my eyes with your beauty be blest,
> No more shall ye sooth my sad bosom to rest.

Fanny had already developed a good memory, and one of

the songs she sang had nearly fifty stanzas. Another, although not so long, states in one of its verses:

> I wish I was a Yankee's wife,
> And then I would have somethin';
> Every fall an ear of corn,
> And now and then a pumpkin!

Fanny, of course, did not write the songs she sang that day, but she felt that the rhyming in some of them lacked a little in perfection. At the age of five there was not much she could do about it.

A farmer was on board taking a cow to market in New York. Toward evening he became somewhat intoxicated. When it came time to milk the cow, he wasn't able to do so. Another passenger volunteered for the chore, and Mrs. Crosby, having recovered from her sea sickness, took the milk and made a large custard to the delight of the crew and passengers. Even the farmer wasn't to the point that he could not recognize a good custard when he tasted it, and he praised Mrs. Crosby's talent in preparing the custard.

The sun dropped behind the hills on the west bank of the great Hudson River, and Fanny went below to her bunk for the night breeze was chilly and she was tired. She fluffed up her pillow and pulled the cover up to her chin. The gentle rocking of the boat and the soft splashing of the waves lulled the blind girl off to dreamland, while the wind and current carried the boat closer and closer to the big city downstream.

> Not alway where the quiet waters flow
> My Saviour leads,
> Nor where the sunlight falls with tender glow
> O'er dewy meads;
> I follow where He will my path should be,
> Content to know but this: He leadeth me.
>
> He from my cradle watched my infant years,
> And chose my way;

O how His wisdom in my life appears
From day to day!

Though oft my journey leads through shadows deep,
I fear no ill;
For, lo, He gives His angels charge to keep
And guard me still.

Sometimes I falter, and the way seems long
To yonder land:
But in His strength made perfect I am strong;
He holds my hand.

3

First Published Poem

Almost a whole day passed while the Crosby party was on the boat traveling from Sing Sing to New York. It was a journey Fanny later made many times by train in less than an hour. When they arrived in New York, they went by carriage to Number Ten Roosevelt Street, the home of a family friend by the name of Jacob Smith. There they rested a few days before visiting Doctors Mott and Delafield.

For a little blind girl who had lived her five years in rural Putnam and Westchester Counties, being in the big city of New York was quite an experience and almost frightening. This was the same year the Erie Canal was opened, running from Albany to Buffalo and thus connecting Lake Erie with the Hudson River. For the first time, boats could travel between Buffalo and New York City—and beyond, of course. When Fanny arrived in New York, people were already preparing for that opening and what it would bring. Prior to the opening of this waterway, it cost about one hundred dollars a ton to move freight from Buffalo to New York City. Soon the cost was to be reduced to about ten dollars a ton. New York, indeed, was a bustling city. People ran to and fro and carriages drawn by horses clopped up and down the cobblestoned streets.

Although this was prior to much of the modern advancement in medicine, Dr. Valentine Mott helped to make part of that medical history. He had studied under Dr. Valentine Seaman, a relative in the New York Hospital, and received his medical degree in 1806 from the medical department of Columbia College. He did postgraduate work in London and

Edinburgh. Returning to New York in 1809, he opened an office and worked there and at Columbia College.

He became known as a bold and original surgeon, and some daring operations gave him worldwide attention. Just seven years prior to Fanny's visit, Dr. Mott was the first to tie the innominate artery, just two inches from the patient's heart. The purpose of the operation was to prevent death by a subclavian aneurism.

Dr. Delafield, too, was a celebrated surgeon, having performed some very successful eye operations. Mrs. Crosby wanted the best for her blind child.

Fanny and her mother arrived at the doctors' office early, and the little girl played with some toys on the floor. When Dr. Mott called Fanny, anxiety was high in both the child and her mother; perhaps more so with the mother, for she understood better the seriousness of the visit.

The two doctors made a thorough examination of Fanny's eyes, and then they went into another room for consultation. On returning, Dr. Mott again took the blind girl on his lap and placed his hands on her head.

"Poor child, I am afraid you will never see again," he said.

Dr. Mott went on to explain to the mother that apparently malpractice on the part of the doctor who had treated her eyes at the age of six weeks had destroyed her sight forever. Surgery would do no good.

It would seem from a human standpoint that bitterness might have overflowed from the heart of young Fanny Crosby, but she never showed any resentment toward the doctor who caused her blindness. In fact, in the true spirit of forgiveness, Fanny wrote of the incident in 1903:

> The poor doctor who had spoiled my eyes, soon disappeared from the neighborhood and we never heard any more about him. He is probably dead, before this time; but if I could ever meet him, I would tell him that unwittingly he did me the greatest favor in the world.

I have heard that this physician never ceased expressing his regret at the occurrence; and that it was one of the sorrows of his life. But if I could meet him now, I would say, "Thank you, thank you"—over and over again—for making me blind, if it was through your agency that it came about!

Why would I not have that doctor's mistake—if a mistake it was—remedied? Well, there are many reasons: and I will tell you some of them.

One is that I know, although it may have been a blunder on the physician's part, it was no mistake of God's. I verily believe it was His intention that I should live my days in physical darkness, so as to be better prepared to sing His praises and incite others so to do. I could not have written thousands of hymns—many of which, if you will pardon me for repeating it, are sung all over the world—if I had been hindered by the distractions of seeing all the interesting and beautiful objects that would have been presented to my notice.

So when five-year-old Fanny, her mother, and her cousin boarded the boat for home, they did so with mixed emotion. Sad indeed were they to know that Fanny would never see the light of day. Yet, there was a certain amount of relief because the child would not have to endure surgery. There was still more consolation in knowing that it must somehow be a part of God's plan for her life.

During the next several months life went on as it had before the New York trip. Fanny still enjoyed the Bible and the poems that were read to her. She soon found that her own rhymes were running through her mind. When she composed a childlike verse, it was published in a county paper. Although there may not be great literary value in it, it does perhaps express a philosophy that stayed with her throughout her life. The poem the young child wrote is entitled "Content," and the lines say:

Oh, what a happy child I am,
Although I cannot see!
I am resolved that in this world
Contented I will be.

How many blessings I enjoy
That other people don't!
So weep or sigh because I'm blind,
I cannot, nor I won't!

Nor was this the extent of her childhood poetry. Not long afterward she wrote a verse she supposed to be humorous. She did not, however, intend this one for publication.

There was a grain mill not far from Fanny's home whose owner had the reputation of not being entirely honest in his dealings with his customers. Fanny wrote of him:

There is a miller in our town,
How dreadful is his case;
I fear unless he does repent
He'll meet with sad disgrace.

A friend of Fanny's mailed the verse to P. T. Barnum, who later became a famous man in the circus business. He was at that time editor of the *Herald of Freedom,* a small paper published in Danbury, Connecticut. To Fanny Crosby's great embarrassment the editor liked the poem and gave it space in his paper. The incident resulted in no serious consequence, but it was a lesson to Fanny to be careful of what she wrote about other people.

Fanny composed a poem on the subject of the wind moaning for the flowers. A friend wrote it down and they mailed it to Fanny's grandfather. Although careful not to say so in the girl's presence, the old gentleman immediately proclaimed his granddaughter a promising poet. A few years later this grandfather walked a round trip of eight miles for a copy of the *New York Herald* that had in it another Fanny Crosby creation.

When Fanny was about nine years old, she and her mother moved to Ridgefield, Connecticut, a few miles from North Salem, New York, and not far from her birthplace at Southeast. Here Mrs. Crosby and Fanny moved into the home of Mrs. Hawley, a member of the prominent Hawley family and ancestor of Joseph Roswell Hawley, who was later a senator from Connecticut. Mrs. Hawley was a devout Christian lady of the Puritan Presbyterian stock. She became another "teacher" to Fanny and evidently was a good one.

Fanny was an apt pupil. Before she was ten years old, in addition to the fine poetry she had memorized, she could quote verbatim the first four books of the Old Testament and the four Gospels of the New Testament!

Fanny and her friends used to gather on the village green and play games. Among these were blind man's bluff, London Bridge, hiding the thimble, and spinning wheel. In one game the boys and girls would make a circle by joining hands. In the center there would be a boy and girl representing a newly married couple, and the group would sing:

> Now, you're married, you must be good,
> And keep your wife in oven-wood.

Among these playmates was a boy by the name of Sylvester Main, who was two or three years older than Fanny. The girls liked Sylvester, for he was not as rough as the others and when other boys became too rowdy, he usually tamed them. Little did Fanny Crosby realize that more than thirty years later she and Sylvester Main would be working together, just as enthusiastically as they played childhood games together.

While Fanny was generally happy and contented, there was one area in her young life that troubled her. From the day that her playmates marched off to school and she couldn't go with them, she knew something was lacking in her life. Other girls and boys her age were learning to read and write. They were learning something of the world outside their immediate vicinity. But for Fanny there was a black wall that separated her from education. Schools for the blind in those days were few, and certainly there were none in rural Putnam and Westchester Counties. At an advanced age Fanny remembered her feelings:

Often, when such circumstances as this made me very blue and depressed, I would creep off alone, kneel down, and ask God if, though blind, I was not one of His children; if in His great world He had not some little place for me; and it often seemed that I could hear Him say, "Do not be discouraged, little girl: you shall someday be happy and useful, even in your blindness." And I would go back among my associates, cheered and encouraged; and feeling that it would not be very long before my life would be full of activity and usefulness.

Fanny remembered kneeling many times by her grandmother's rocking chair and sending up her humble petition, "Dear Lord, please show me how I can learn like other children." It was a prayer uttered perhaps more often than any other prayer in her entire childhood.

While she waited for the answer, life went on as usual and with the exception of schooling, her activities, her joys, and her temptations were not much different from those of other children her age.

Mrs. Hawley, like Fanny, loved flowers. Many kinds of flowers grew in profusion in her yard. Several varieties of roses were among them. Mrs. Hawley made it plain to Fanny that she could pick them whenever she chose—any of them, that is, except the white variety, of which there was only one bush.

One afternoon Fanny and a playmate were playing in the yard and gathered a few of those roses that Mrs. Hawley had given her permission to gather. The friend, however, thought the white ones looked better and urged Fanny to pick one.

"Mrs. Hawley doesn't wish us to pick them," Fanny replied, but the friend insisted and Fanny yielded to the temptation.

Mrs. Hawley, who was sitting at the window, observed the transgression of her rule, but said nothing at the time. Later in the afternoon she called Fanny to her and said, "Fanny, do you know who picked the pretty white rose from the bush yonder?"

"No, madam," Fanny answered meekly. Mrs. Hawley said nothing more of the incident, but that evening when it was time to read to Fanny, somehow the story of Ananias and Sapphira was selected. And from that hour Fanny Crosby resolved to obey Mrs. Hawley's rules and to tell no more falsehoods.

As Fanny grew from a child to a young teenager, much of her time was spent in sewing, knitting, and other household duties. She continued, of course, her study of the Bible. Her love for poetry and music increased, and she learned to play the guitar. When she was about fourteen, Fanny and her mother moved back to Westchester County. There the mother found more suitable employment and they were nearer Southeast, where her grandmother lived.

On an afternoon in November, 1834, Fanny's mother called her. As Fanny met her mother at the gate, she heard the rustling of a paper in her hand. The blind child could not see the expression on her mother's face and thus had no clue as to the nature of the message.

Could it be news of the illness or death of a loved one, she wondered.

4
Second Trip to New York

Fanny Crosby grew up with the knowledge that her loving heavenly Father wanted the best for his children. She was subject to disappointment, sadness, and heartache, just as all people are, but she believed that God allowed nothing to happen to his own that was not for their good—either in this life or the next. She loved to quote Romans 8:28: "We know that all things work together for good to them that love God, to them who are the called according to his purpose."

So even at the age of fourteen, Fanny was able to cope with most disappointments that came her way. But on that November afternoon when she met her mother at the gate, there was a surprise in store for her. The letter was not from a relative or a friend announcing sickness or death. It was from the New York Institution for the Blind. Mrs. Crosby told her that arrangements had been made for her to attend the school in New York City.

"Oh, thank God!" Fanny cried with joy, "He has answered my prayer, just as I knew he would!"

As thrilled as Fanny was at the thought of an education, at this early date she had little idea of the influence the school and the people there would have upon her. And certainly she had no thought of the help she would be to the school, especially during the crucial years just after its opening. In those days there were few schools for the blind. Many people looked upon persons with any sort of physical handicap as helpless and unfortunate burdens to themselves and their families. If a school such as the New York Institution for the Blind was to survive, people in responsible positions in government, the general public, and parents with handicapped children must be informed of certain facts. One of these facts was that most handicapped children, given proper education, training, encouragement, and opportunity could be useful and happy citizens. To this end, Fanny Crosby was to perform an important part.

The New York Institution for the Blind was established in 1831, and opened March 15, 1832, about three years prior to Fanny's enrollment. During those three years there had been a total of only thirty pupils. She was to be number thirty-one.

The school was founded on Ninth Avenue by Dr. John Dennison Russ, Dr. Samuel Akerly, and Mr. Samuel Wood. Doctor Russ graduated in arts from Yale College in 1823, and received his medical degree from the same school in 1825. He spent a year working in hospitals in Europe and returned to New York City to practice medicine. Concerned for the Greeks and their independence in 1827, the doctor went to Greece with a shipload of food and supplies furnished by various American citizens. There he distributed the food and helped to organize hospitals. After three years, he returned to New York and resumed his practice.

Epidemics of cholera and ophthalmia occurred in New York during the years of 1830 and 1831. The latter infection rendered many children blind, and Dr. Russ became vitally interested in their welfare.

So the school was begun with only three pupils. Dr. Russ himself served as teacher and later as superintendent.

Today the school has been in operation for almost a century and a half and has the distinction of being the oldest such school in the western hemisphere. Its present address is 999 Pelham Parkway, New York, New York, 10469. Its name has been slightly modified to New York Institute for the Education of the Blind.

So from that November day in 1834, when Fanny learned the good news, until her departure for school on the third of March, 1835, she lived in anticipation of one of the greatest things that had ever happened to her. At the same time, she was sad, because she would leave her mother and the friends she loved.

"What will you do without me?" her mother asked, perhaps trying to prepare her ahead of time for the shock of leaving home. "You have never been away from home more than two weeks at one time in your whole life."

"As much as I love you, Mother," Fanny answered, "I am willing to make any sacrifice to acquire an education."

"You are right, my child," the mother answered, "and I am very glad you have the chance to go." But notwithstanding the many things a loving mother can do, it's difficult indeed for her to pretend joy at the thought of being separated from her child. And the tremor in Mrs. Crosby's voice betrayed the words she spoke.

A few years afterward, Fanny wrote:

> I'll think of thee at that soft hour,
> When fade the parting hues of day;
> And on each grove and woodland bower
> The balmy gales of summer play.
>
> When night around her mantle throws,
> And stars illume the deep blue sea,
> When wearied nature seeks repose,
> Oh, then, I'll dream, I'll dream of thee.
>
> When from the East the morning breaks;
> And night's dark shadows glide away;
> When Nature from her slumber wakes
> To hail with joy the opening day.
>
> When sweetly bursting on the ear,
> The tuneful warbler's note of glee,
> I'll fondly fancy thou art near
> To touch the light guitar for me.

On March 3, 1835, before the roosters started crowing and while the neighbors' houses were dark and quiet, candlelight shone from the windows of the Crosby cottage. The smell of birchwood came from the wood-burning cookstove and Mrs. Crosby busied herself preparing breakfast for Fanny, who was still asleep.

Transportation had improved somewhat since Fanny's first trip to New York. There was a stage that ran by her home on its way to Norwalk, Connecticut, on Long Island Sound. When it was nearly time for the stage to arrive, Mrs. Crosby called her daughter to breakfast.

The thought of going away unnerved Fanny, and she dressed with trembling fingers. She tried to swallow a few bites of breakfast, but the food refused to go down. On hearing the stage, she hurried from the house for fear she would break down completely if she waited to bid her mother goodbye. Fanny sat for an hour without saying a word beside the lady who was accompanying her to New York. The lady did her best to cheer Fanny.

Fanny's throat muscles felt as though they would burst. She knew a good cry would bring relief, but at the moment the tears would not come.

Finally, her companion said, "Fanny, if you don't want to go to New York, we will get out at the next station, and take the returning stage home. Your mother will be lonesome without you, anyway."

At that, Fanny broke into convulsive sobs. Then she felt better. When she could control her voice again, she said, "No, I will go on to New York."

So the stage rumbled on to Norwalk. There Fanny and the lady she was with boarded a steamer for New York, where the blind girl would seek a different kind of light from that sought on the previous journey. She hoped the results of this trip would be less disappointing.

> The deep blue sky, serenely light,
> On which your eyes with rapture gaze;
> Where stars unveil their mellow bright,
> And God His wondrous power displays.

The gushing fount, whose glassy breast,
Reflects the parting hues of day,
Nature in robes of verdure drest,
The opening buds, the flowerets gay.

The lofty hills, the greenwood bowers,—
Though fair these rural scenes appear,
On them to gaze must ne'er be ours:
These orbs, alas! they cannot cheer.

But, ye, instruction's nobler light;
Sheds on our mental eye its ray;
We hail its beams with new delight,
And bid each gloomy thought away.

To us the Lord kind friends has given,
Whose names we ever shall revere,
Recorded in the book of heaven,
Shall their munificence appear.

But, while our sunny moments fly,
Unsullied by a shade of care,
For those, like us bereft, we sigh,
And wish they, too, our joys might share.

5
The Superintendent's Lecture

The quiet motion of the steamship soothed Fanny Crosby's nerves, and when she reached the harbor in New York City she was feeling somewhat better. She and her companion made their way to the home of friends, where Fanny remained for three days. Then on March 7, 1835, Fanny was driven to the New York Institution for the Blind on Ninth Avenue.

When Fanny arrived, the teachers tried to cheer her up, but in spite of their efforts, she broke down again and cried. The matron, a motherly Quaker lady, put her arms around the blind girl and said, "Fanny, I guess thee has never been away from home before."

"No, ma'am," Fanny replied. The lady led her to the room where she would sleep and introduced her to some other girls. Fanny sat on a trunk beside one of the other girls and the two talked about everything but home and family until bedtime. Being with another person who she could identify with seemed to take Fanny's mind off herself. During the pleasant conversation, her tears dried and she soon almost forgot they had even flowed at all.

Fanny enjoyed her studies and did well in them with one exception, arithmetic. She referred to it as "the monster," and although she tried desperately, it seemed she just could not learn the subject. She said of it:

I have never been a very good hater, even when the best material was provided for the purpose; but I found myself adept at the art of loathing, when it came to the Science of

Numbers. The culinary poet who in a fit of dyspepsia exuded the statement,

> I loathe, abhor, detest, despise
> Those pastry-wrecks, dried apple pies,

had a parodist in me. I could not agree with him concerning the article of food in question, for I like almost everything that a good cook can send to the table; but I *could* say, at that time,

> I loathe, abhor, it makes me sick
> To hear the word arithmetic!

Two days after her first assignment in the multiplication tables, Dr. Russ came in and asked the girl, who was instructing Fanny in the tables, "Well, Anna, has our pupil learned the multiplication tables yet?"

"Not quite," the girl replied.

"Well, then," the superintendent continued, "I shall come again tomorrow; and if Fanny Crosby does not know them at that time, I shall put her on the mantle." Fanny took him seriously, and through sheer determination and lengthy effort, she memorized them.

She continued her struggle in the subject until she came to long division, and there her patience failed. She decided that she simply could not learn arithmetic. She told her teacher, "I suppose you regard me as a very inattentive pupil."

"No, I do not, for you can never learn mathematics," the teacher said. "Let us go to the superintendent and tell him so."

A conference was held and it was decided that after the basic requirement was met, Fanny would be excused from further work in the subject. This relieved the blind girl, and even in her old age she could recite a verse printed in one of her early arithmetic books:

> Multiplication is vexation,
> Division is as bad;
> The rule of three puzzles me,
> And fractions make me mad.

In her other subjects, the story was different. Besides the Bible, Fanny's favorite studies were history, philosophy, the small portion of science available then, and English, and she learned to recite verbatim most of *Brown's Grammar*. She loved these subjects, and her remarkable memory enabled her to do well in them.

It was perhaps fortunate for Fanny that John D. Russ was superintendent of the school. Doctor Russ was instrumental in the invention of the phonetic alphabet and the development of embossed letters for the blind. He was a lover of poetry and while he was in Greece had become intimately associated with Lord Byron. Much of his time in the classroom was devoted to reading the best of poetry to the students.

"We used to read the *Bible, Pilgrim's Progress, The Ancient Mariner,* and other literary classics in the raised letters," Fanny related, "but our daily lessons were received directly from our teachers, and they had an excellent plan of instruction. Selections would be read to us two or three times, and then we were all expected to be able to answer minute questions about them in the language of the original. The following morning we were required to tell the story again, this time, however, in our own words."

Poetry was studied in depth. Among Fanny's favorite poets were Thomas Moore, Horatius Bonar, James Montgomery, Longfellow, Tennyson, Byron, Whittier, Willis, Wesley, and Morris. And it wasn't long until her own muse was restless for release.

She once wrote a long poem she called "The Poets Corner." In it were fourteen verses, thirteen of which were dedicated to specific poets and written much in the style of each respective poet. Of Longfellow, she said:

> Sweet Laughing Water! dear to me
> That Indian tale will ever be,
> So blent with every watching art
> That lures the sense and charms the heart.

And of William Cullen Bryant she asked:

> Didst hear thy summons when it came,
> When soft the angel breathed thy name?
> Didst round thee fold thy drapery white,
> And, bidding all the world good night,
> Beneath that star from heaven that beams,
> Didst lay thee down to pleasant dreams?

Of J. G. Whittier she said:

> I would be Snow Bound many a day
> If I could sit and hear thee say,
> "Of all sad words of tongue or pen
> The saddest are these, it might have been."

And the long poem concluded:

> You from whose garners I have gleaned
> Such precious fruit, the task has seemed
> So pleasant that my humble pen
> Would fain resume its work again;
> In your bright realms 'twere bliss to stay:
> But time forbids, and I obey.

Fanny's early efforts at poetry were praised by her peers and somewhat condescendingly so by her teachers. When two of the teachers become romantically interested in one another, to the amusement of her school chums, Fanny wrote:

> Say, dearest, wilt thou roam with me
> To Scotland's bonny bowers,
> Where purest fountains gently glide,
> And bloom the sweetest flowers.
> Ah Martha, may we soon retire
> Unto some pleasant cot,

Where love and joy forever dwell
And sorrow is forgot.

There in the gentle summer eve
We'll watch the murmuring streams;
The moon shall fondly cheer our hearts
With its majestic beams.
Then, let the wintery blasts appear,
And all the flowers decay;
We'll sit beside the cheerful fire,
And sing dull care away.

Reflecting on her school days Fanny said:

Fortunately for me our teachers read us some of the best
of modern poets; and they inspired me to more determined
efforts to improve whatever little gift I possessed by nature.
Some of my schoolmates, however, took my crude efforts as
models to be imitated; and two or three of them actually
tried to compose poetry on their own account. From time
to time they would make sorry work of meters and rhymes;
and almost invariable, sooner or later, they would come to
me for aid with the careful injunction, 'You mustn't tell
anyone for all the world.' Thus I was sworn to secrecy; they
were admitted to the poetic workshop, and actual labor
began. We fitted and joined; smoothed and planed; mea-
sured and moulded, until by the joint effort of three or four
people something was produced that our childish fancy took
to be good verses. They were not; and years afterward all of
us had many a hearty laugh over these youthful experi-
ments.

Not long after Fanny enrolled at the Institution, Dr. Russ
left the school and for a few months the office of superintendent was unfilled. During Fanny's second year in the school,
in 1836, Mr. Silas Jones became the new superintendent.
Doctor Anthony Reiff came as a teacher and, according to
Fanny Crosby, was loved by the students and remained at the

Institution for forty years. Fanny especially enjoyed his singing classes.

A new school building was completed and on a crisp
November morning in 1837, the cornerstone was laid. The
mayor, common council, and many other prominent citizens
were there for the dedication. For the occasion Fanny wrote
the words and Mr. Reiff the music to a march. A part of it
states:

> This day may every bosom feel
> A thrill of pleasure and delight;
> The scenes will in our memories dwell,
> When Time shall wing his rapid flight.
> May the great Being who surveys
> The countless acts by mortals done,
> Behold with an approving eye
> The structure which is now begun.

Fanny continued to write verse, mostly for the entertainment of her friends, and occasionally for special events, such
as the one just mentioned.

Later Fanny wrote:

Before 1840 my friends had nearly spoiled me with their
praises. At least I began to feel my own importance as a
poet a little too much . . . . One morning after breakfast I
was summoned to the office; and, thinking he [Mr. Jones]
would ask me for a poem, or perhaps give me a word of
commendation, as he sometimes did, I obeyed at once. But
instead of more praise and a new commission to write
verses, I found a plain talk awaiting me.

It was an impressive occasion, and I remember what Mr.
Jones said almost word for word:

"Fanny, I am sorry you have allowed yourself to be
carried away by what others said about your verses. True,
you have written a number of poems of real merit; but how
far do they fall short of the standard that you might attain.
Shun a flatterer, Fanny, as you would a viper; for no true

friend would deceive you with words of flattery. Remember that whatever talent you possess belongs wholly to God; and that you ought to give Him the credit for all that you do."

Mr. Jones was a fine teacher of the young; and he knew just what was best in my particular case. After giving me a little more advice, he said,

"Now, we will reconstruct the fabric—but on a different plan. You have real poetic talent; yet it is crude and undeveloped; and if your talent ever amounts to much, you must polish and smooth your verses so that they may be of more value. Store your mind with useful knowledge; and the time may come, sooner or later, when you will attain the goal toward which you have already made some progress."

Then the dear man said to me, "Fanny, have I wounded your feelings?" Something within me bore witness that Mr. Jones spoke the truth; and so I answered,

"No, sir, on the contrary, you have talked to me like a father, and I thank you very much for it."

Such advice, of course, is never pleasant to a poet or writer—and probably to no one else for that matter—but Fanny accepted it in the light in which it was given. She remembered it throughout her life as advice "worth more than the price of rubies."

6
A New Family

Mr. Jones' rebuke probably was not to imply that Fanny could not or should not become a poet. Rather, it was a caution against egotism. Also, he may have felt, as her teachers seemed to believe, that the world was full of would-be poets of which the majority will never make the grade. In short, the faculty apparently was of the opinion that Fanny Crosby's poetic attempts were distracting her from her studies and hampering her education, the object of her being at the Institution.

Fanny remembered the advice and was determined to curb any self-pride that might arise. She could not, however, curb the desire to write, and she continued to do so. Some of her teachers began confiscating her poems and trying in other ways to discourage her. Finally the second summons came to return to Mr. Jones' office and another effort was made to deter Fanny's writing.

"You are not to write a line of poetry for three months," he demanded.

This came as perhaps the greatest shock of Fanny's young life. Completely disillusioned and bewildered, she tried to concentrate on her studies and abide by the superintendent's order. Notwithstanding a great effort was extended toward her classes, but instead of improving, her grades became poorer still. Within a month and a half she was in danger of failing her subjects, and again the superintendent called for her.

"Fanny, what is the trouble with your lessons?" he asked. "The teachers report that you do not recite as well as you did during last term. Are you ill?"

"I find it impossible to keep my mind on my lessons, for poetry occupies my thoughts in spite of all efforts to think of other things. I cannot help it."

"Well," Mr. Jones said, "write as much as you like, but pay a little more attention to the morning lectures."

During those days phrenology, the practice of studying the human skull to determine character and mental capacity, was popularly accepted by many people. Soon after Superintendent Jones gave permission for Fanny to resume her poetry writing, a notable phrenologist from Scotland, and more recently from Boston, was touring the area of New York. He visited the New York Institution for the Blind and examined the craniums of the pupils.

Sitting in the classroom near Fanny was a boy that many in the school looked upon as a child prodigy. According to reports that came to Fanny, he could listen to two persons talking to him at the same time, and then, while singing a song could calculate the number of seconds in their ages, having, of course, first been informed the years, months, and days. When Dr. Combe, the phrenologist, placed his hands upon the boy's head, he exclaimed, "Why, here is a splendid mathematician! Some day you will hear from him." (Fanny recalled some sixty years later that the doctor had been right on the first count, but as for the second, the boy never did become famous. In fact, after he left school she never heard of him again.)

When the doctor came to Fanny and placed his hands on her head, he said, "Why, here is a poet! Give her every advantage that she can have; let her hear the best books and converse with the best writers, and she will make her mark in the world."

Fanny may not have had a great amount of faith in the ability of Dr. Combe to accurately predict her future, but one thing is certain. At this stage she welcomed a word of encouragement from anyone—even a phrenologist.

From that day, when Fanny Crosby felt the urge to write a poem, she wrote it. And in so doing, her scholastic standing improved and she was once again an apt pupil. Hamilton Murray, who at that time was a member of the board of managers of the school, took an interest in her and her love of poetry. He read to the blind girl the classics by the hour and helped her commit long passages to memory. For practice he would sometimes give her a poem from a notable poet and have her write one on a different subject but in the same style and form. One of these poems says:

> O could we wake from sorrow,
> Were it all a changeful dream like this:
> To cast aside like an untimely garment of the morn:
> Could the long fever of the soul be cooled
> By a sweet breath from nature,
> How lightly were the spirit reconciled.

Fanny Crosby's parody states:

> O could we with the gloomy shades of night
> Chase the dark clouds of sorrow from the brow;
> Could pure affection feel no withering blight,
> But heart to heart in one sweet tie be linked,
> How were the soul content to fold her wings,
> And dwell forever in such loveliness.

Much of Fanny's writing during her student years was poems for addresses to be made when some prominent figure would visit the school, or during the dedication of a building. Many of the titles indicate the nature of the poem: "Address to Rev. Dr. Hewitt," "Address to General Bertrand," "On the Departure of a Teacher," "On the Death of General Harrison," "Dedication of the Chapel," and so on. The words of the latter are as follows:

> Oh! thou omniscient, omnipresent Lord!
> Invisible, eternal God of all!
> The vast creation trembles at thy word

And at thy footstool nations prostrate fall.
Thy throne is fixed above the starry frame;
Yet thou, in earthly temples lov'st to dwell.
The humble spirit thou wilt not disdain—
The wounded heart, thy balm divine dost heal.

Father, we humbly supplicate thy grace;—
May thy benignant smiles to us be given;
Thy blessing rest upon this sacred place;
Thine earthly house—we trust, the gate of
    heaven.

Here will we listen to thy Holy Word;
Light to our path, oh! may its precepts be;
Here shall the voice of praise, and prayer be
    heard—
Ourselves, our all, we dedicate to Thee.

Protect, oh Lord! the dwelling of the blind,
And to its guardians, aid divine impart;
Oh! make us to thy holy will resigned,
Let love and union reign in every heart.

Accept our songs of gratitude and praise;
Soon may we tune the golden lyres above,
And with cherubic legions, sweetly raise,
The ceaseless anthems of eternal love.

Fanny was the only child of John and Mercy Crosby and often thought how fortunate a child was who had brothers and sisters. Her father had died when she was an infant, and she therefore had no brothers or sisters. Early in 1838, Fanny received a letter from her mother saying she soon would marry Thomas Morris, a widower with three children. His wife had died when the third child was six days old. On February 4, 1838, three years after Fanny came to the school, her mother, Mercy Crosby, and Thomas Morris were united in marriage.

Father, Saviour, Holy Spirit
Bless these wedded souls we pray;
Make their future bright and cloudless
As a rosy, summer day.

And when evening shadows gather
When their harvest work is done,
May they both go home rejoicing
At the setting of the sun.

7
Distinguished Visitors

Much of Fanny's early writing was of a civic or patriotic nature. Often upon the death of a war hero or a prominent government official she would write a poem in commemoration of the event. For example, when President William Henry Harrison died on April 4, 1841, just one month after taking office, Fanny Crosby wrote of the untimely death. A portion of the poem is given here:

> He is gone: in death's cold arms he sleeps.
> Our President, our hero brave,
> While fair Columbia o'er him weeps,
> And chants a requiem at his grave;
> Her sanguine hopes are blighted now,
> And weeds of sorrow veil her brow.
>
> Ah, Indiana, where is he,
> Who once thy sons to battle led?
> The red man quailed beneath his eye,
> And from his camp disheartened fled.
> With steady hand he bent the bow
> And laid the warlike savage low.
>
> The forest with his praises rung,
> His fame was echoed far and wide—
> With loud hurrah his name was sung,
> Columbia's hero and her pride.
> The tuneful harp is now unstrung
> And on the drooping willow hung.

The *New York Herald* published the poem and as was mentioned earlier, Fanny's Grandfather Crosby, who still lived at Southeast, walked eight miles to secure a copy of his granddaughter's poem.

In 1841 Dr. Peter D. Vroom succeeded Mr. Jones as superintendent of the New York Institution for the Blind. One day in the spring of the following year, Dr. Vroom came into the room where Fanny was and announced that President Tyler, who had become president of the United States upon the death of President Harrison, was in the reception room. With him were the mayor and common council.

"Now, give me ten or fifteen minutes," Fanny said, "and I shall have the best welcome that I can prepare in so short a time." And within a few minutes she appeared on the stage before the group, recited her specially written poem, sang a song, and concluded by reading a song she had written for the previous Fourth of July. A part of the latter song declares:

> And this the glad song of our Nation shall be,
> Hurrah for John Tyler and liberty's tree.

Although Fanny was in close contact and became intimate friends with some prominent people, her love for them was no greater than her love for her schoolmates, many of whom became her dear friends. Among her early schoolmates who became lifelong friends were Imogene Hart, Cynthia Bullock, Catherine Kennedy, Anna Smith, Mary Mattox, and Alice Holmes. There were others with whom Fanny lost contact after they left the school and she wrote of them:

> Where are the friends of my youth,
> Oh, where are those treasured ones gone?

To her friend, Cynthia Bullock, Fanny wrote:

To a Friend

> When wilt thou think of me?
> When the vesper bell is pealing,
> And its distant sounds are stealing

Softly on the listening ear,
Breathing music sweet and clear;
When in prayer on bended knee,
Wilt thou then remember me?

When wilt thou think of me?
When the twilight fades away,
And the bird hath ceased its lay,
And the quiet evening shade
Lingers in the silent glade;
When thy thoughts are wandering free,
Wilt thou then remember me?

When wilt thou think of me?
When thy gentle heart is crushed,
And its sweetest tones are hushed;
When upon some faithful breast,
Thou wouldst lull thy grief to rest,
Then in whispers soft to thee
I would say, remember me.

Imogene Hart became a singer, musician, poet, and writer in her own right. Alice Holmes, perhaps close to Fanny over a longer period of time than any of her other schoolmates, became a prolific poet. Besides the poems that appeared in various newspapers and magazines, she published two volumes of poetry. Much of her time not spent in writing was occupied with knitting or other needle work. It has been said that although completely blind Miss Holmes' touch was so sensitive that she could sort boxes of yarn according to color. On Miss Holmes' ninety-second birthday a news reporter visited the blind woman and wrote of her: She was sorting over a basket full of various colored wools when the representative of the *Herald* called upon her. How she can tell one color from another is the secret of her well-trained fingers.

One of the first notables that Fanny entertained at the school was Henri Gratien Bertrand. After the famous Napoleon Bonaparte's defeat and exile to Saint Helena, Marshal Bertrand followed him to the desolate island and there was his constant companion until Napoleon's death in 1821. He subsequently wrote his memoirs, *Napoleon at St. Helena.*

When Marshal Bertrand visited the school, Fanny recited a poem that she had written in his honor, a part of which states:

> When by those he loved deserted,
> Thine was still a faithful heart;
> Thou wert proud to share the exile
> Of the hapless Bonaparte.
>
> Like an angel, whispering comfort,
> Still in sickness thou wert nigh;
> And when life's last scenes were over,
> Tears of anguish dimmed thine eye.

One of the first trips Fanny made in behalf of the school, and "one of the most enjoyable," Fanny said, was one made on a lowly canal boat via the Erie Canal. The journey took her and a group of other students all the way to Buffalo and Niagara Falls, with frequent stops along the way to entertain the public and impress upon it the accomplishments of the school.

At Niagara Falls Fanny could not see the mighty rushing, plunging river. "But," she said, "I could still hear the trumpet-voice of this king of cataracts, proclaiming the power of the Almighty hand. I could feel the fresh breezes that sprang from the bosom of the whirling waters; I could (sweetest thought of all) enjoy the enjoyment of my friends who could see, and listen to their animated descriptions."

It was a trip the students were sad to know must end, and when they finally returned to the school, they talked of it for months—yes, even years—afterward.

People visited the school frequently and it was usually Fanny Crosby who guided their tour of the Institution. She enjoyed relating to others the amusing incidents connected with the tours. On one occasion a lady visitor, thoughtless perhaps, asked her how the blind managed to find their mouths with a spoon or fork. The time being well past Fanny's lunch hour, she told the lady that if she would provide the food, she would be happy to give her a demonstration.

Another incident which always caused Fanny to chuckle upon recalling was when a group of students, along with the music teacher, stayed at a hotel. The teacher, Mr. Anthony Reiff, had perfect vision. The hotel clerk asked him, "How long have you been this way?"

"All my life," Mr. Reiff replied, and the clerk led him to his room.

Fanny always looked forward to summer vacations when she could visit her family. Often a group of her friends would accompany her home, where they, too, were heartily welcomed.

During the school months, though, Fanny rarely saw her folks and had to be content with corresponding by letter, and one day in 1839 one such letter came that was extra special and gladdened the blind girl's heart. Fanny Crosby had a baby sister, and the parents named the baby Wilhemina.

8
Before Congress

Fanny did not really have an opportunity to get acquainted with her little sister, for when Wilhemina Morris was five months old, the death angel came and took her. And although Fanny was saddened on receiving the message, she accepted it as God's will. She at once mailed the following letter and poem to her mother and stepfather:

"The impression that her death has made upon my mind is a deep one; but this event teaches me a lesson, which, I trust, I never shall forget. Once I looked forward to future years when she would be not only a comfort to you but also to myself, but these fond hopes are blighted. Let us not repine, but cheerfully submit to the will of Heaven.

> She's gone, ah yes, her lovely form
> Too soon has ceased to bloom,
> An emblem of the fragile flower
> That blossoms for the tomb.
>
> Yet, mother, check that starting tear,
> That trembles in thine eye;
> And thou, kind father, cease to mourn,
> Suppress that heaving sigh.
>
> She's gone, and thou, dear aunt, no more
> Wilt watch her cradle bed,
> She slumbers in the peaceful tomb,
> But weep not for the dead.
>
> Kind uncle, thou art grieving too,
> Thy tears in thought I see;

Ah, never will her infant hand
Be stretched again to thee.

She's gone, yet why should we repine,
Our darling is at rest:
Her cherub spirit now reclines
On her Redeemer's breast.

Within a few years, however, two other sisters were born and lived long lives, and Fanny shared many happy experiences with them. Their names were Julia and Carolyn, or Carrie, as Fanny affectionately called her.

When a group of Fanny's school friends went home with her on one summer vacation, one of the fellows in the group came down with a cold. All sorts of folk remedies were common then and one Fanny's mother had heard about was the practice of rubbing salt into the scalp. Having no other medication in the house, and unable to think of any harm it could do, Mrs. Morris prepared to administer the remedy. The boy resisted but she insisted and upon applying the first handful she discovered he was wearing a hairpiece and understood his reluctance to the treatment. Fanny said later that it was not easy to tell who was the more embarrassed, Mrs. Morris or the young man, but being unable to think of a remedy for embarrassment or baldness, the practice of the medicine was dropped and the cold, at least, cleared up within a day or two.

Fanny's sisters, when they were old enough, looked forward to her homecoming just as much as Fanny enjoyed going. For weeks prior to such visits, they saved their pennies to buy sweetmeats to share with Sister Fanny. They both enjoyed normal eyesight and would take Fanny on guided tours of the meadows, pastures, hills, streams, and sometimes the stores in town.

Birthdays were special and when her mother's would come each year, Fanny always sent a poem, written just for her. Not only was this true during the daughter's school years, but it continued as long as her mother lived. On her mother's eighty-second birthday, Fanny wrote:

> How pleasant to look on a brow like hers,
> With hardly a trace of care;
> How cheerful the light of her beaming eye,
> As she sits in her easy chair.
>
> So little the change in her dear, kind face
> We scarce can believe it true
> That she numbers today her four score years,
> Four score years and two.
>
> Her winter of age, though the snowflakes fell,
> Has never been dark and drear,
> She moves with the vigor of younger feet,
> And her mind is bright and clear.
>
> She merrily talks of the olden time,
> Of the friends in youth she knew:
> She is sprightly and gay, though she numbers today
> Her four score years and two.
>
> And now as we come with our birthday gifts,
> When she views them o'er and o'er,
> And the earnest "God bless you, my children dear,"
> Is breathed from her lips once more.
>
> We think how devoted our mother's love,
> What a sunshine of joy she gives,
> And we feel as we tenderly kiss her cheek,
> What a comfort that still she lives!

During the fall semester in 1843, Fanny's health was poor, and when it was announced that a number of students were to go to Washington, D. C. in January, she wondered if she would be able to be in that group. By the end of the year, however, her condition had improved somewhat and Dr. Clements, the school physician, decided the trip would not be harmful. "In fact," he said, "the trip South might do you some good." The Board of Managers, along with William Boggs, who had succeeded Dr. Vroom as superintendent, gave their permission. There was a stipulation in the agreement. It was that Dr. Clements accompany the group. Doctor Clements agreed to go and Fanny, of course, was pleased that the doctor would be along. But when she learned the purpose of the trip was to impress upon the legislators the absolute need of schools for the blind in every state and that it was Fanny Crosby who was to address a joint session of Congress, she wondered if she might need more than a doctor to give her the courage she needed.

As the time approached, the thrill of the trip took on greater dimensions and her fear subsided to some extent. When the group finally arrived in Washington and the great moment arrived, Fanny Crosby mustered all the courage she could and stood before her audience of distinguished men. She recited one of her longest poems—one written specifically for the occasion. When she concluded there was a terrifying silence, which probably lasted no longer than a second but to the blind girl it seemed like several minutes. She felt that the legislators were displeased, but when a thunder of applause burst forth it actually frightened her.

When members of the audience asked for another poem, there was a hasty consultation between the Board of Managers and Dr. Clements.

"Don't let her try it," one of the managers said, "tell them that she is not strong enough." Dr. Clements then asked Fanny if she had another poem and if she felt well enough to recite it. "Yes," she answered, "I will recite another poem, for I may never get a chance to address such a famous audience again." She walked back upon the platform and recited a poem she had written and published the previous year. It was one in memory of the Honorable Hugh S. Lagare, Secretary of State, who died suddenly while going with President Tyler to attend the program of laying the cornerstone of the Bunker Hill monument. A few of the lines are:

Farewell, esteemed departed one, farewell,
Deep solem tones have pealed thy funeral knell,—
Thou to the grave art gone. Sweet be thy rest!
For angels guard the relics of the blest.

Hark, hark, thy requiem floats upon the ear,
So deeply sad. We pause; we weep to hear.
Ye patriot sons of fair Columbia's shore,
A brilliant star has set, to shine no more.

Weep, oh, Columbia, o'er his lonely grave,
Then let the cypress, sorrow's emblem, wave,
The mournful breezes sigh, wild flowerets bloom,
And breathe their fragrance o'er his hallowed tomb.

Fanny Crosby could not see them, but tears welled in the eyes of many in the great audience.

In the audience was the sister of the man in whose honor the poem was written. She had read the poem in the paper and on learning that the students were to be in Washington, she made arrangements to be there, too, and to meet the blind girl who wrote the poem.

Fanny was told that she was the first woman ever to appear before Congress. Nor was that her only appearance. In 1847 the group from the New York Institution for the Blind joined with a school from Boston and one from Philadelphia to present their petitions once again to a joint session of Congress.

On this trip Fanny met a girl whose ability she marveled at. Laura Dewey Bridgman, nine years younger than she, was born in Hanover, New Hampshire, in 1829. When she was two years old, a fever destroyed her sight, hearing, and sense of smell. There was at that time a Dr. Howe working in the Perkins Institution in Boston and he took the girl into his care, hoping to break the threefold barrier that separated her from the rest of the world. The blind girl learned to read embossed letters by touch. Then Dr. Howe found that she could communicate her thoughts by touching a board containing metal letters of the alphabet. Within two years Laura was able to take up the studies of geography, algebra, and history. And she learned to do needlework and various household chores. She went on to become a teacher of the blind and deaf.

On the night that Fanny met the blind and deaf girl in Washington, Laura shook hands with six congressmen, whose names were written on her palm. In a few minutes the same group of men passed before her, but in different order. To their amazement, as well as Fanny, Laura Bridgman identified all six men.

During this tour Fanny also had the privilege of hearing John Quincy Adams' last speech. The former President died the following year, in 1848. Fanny proudly remembered his speech on the subject of the Smithsonian Institute and cherished the thought that the aged man had clasped her hand in a sincere and friendly handshake.

On these two trips to the nation's capital, Fanny met other distinguished men, such as Stephen A. Douglas, Andrew Johnson, and Jefferson Davis. She visited President James K. Polk, too, but felt she already knew him as a warm, personal friend, for he had previously visited the New York Institution for the Blind. On that occasion she had welcomed him with a poem, two lines of which state:

> We welcome not a monarch with a crown upon his brow,
> Before no haughty tyrant as suppliants we bow.

Fanny felt that these lines portrayed the simplicity of the man she wrote about. When she talked with the President in Washington, she found that he had not forgotten.

"Well, Miss Crosby," he asked, "have you made any poetry since I saw you last year?"

"Yes, Sir," she answered. "I have composed a song and dedicated it to you."

This had been Fanny's carefully guarded secret and she surprised those in her delegation, as well as the President. He asked her to take his arm, and the group proceeded to the music room for an impromptu recital.

On the trip back to New York, Mr. J. F. Chamberlain, who had become superintendent of the school on the resignation of Mr. Boggs, asked Fanny, "Have you heard my poem, 'Away to the Prairie'?" When Fanny answered that she had not, he recited it to her:

> Away to the prairie, up, up and away,
> Where the bison are roaming, the deer are at play;
> From the wrongs that surround us, the home of our rest,
> Let us seek on the wide, rolling plains of the West.
>
> Away to the prairie, where the pioneer's lay
> Is echoed afar on the breezes; away!
>
> To the wide, rolling plains of the West let us hie,
> Where the clear river's bosom immirrors the sky,
> On whose banks stands the warrior so brave,
> Whose bark hath alone left a curl on the wave.
>
> Yes, away to the prairie, whose bosom, though wild,
> Is unstrained by oppression, by fraud undefiled;
> From the wrongs that surround us, the home of our rest,
> Let us seek on the wide, rolling plains of the West.

Fanny asked him to hum the melody. "There is none," he said, "But why don't you write one?" Fanny did compose music for the words Mr. Chamberlain had written, and the song was popular at the school for many years. It, as well as many others, was used in sing-alongs whenever a group gathered at the school, and it was usually Fanny Crosby that furnished the accompaniment on the guitar, piano, or chapel organ.

In 1848, President Polk again visited the Institution, and Fanny Crosby had the honor of dining with him and showing him about the school and grounds. When they were about to go for a stroll among the lofty trees, it came to Fanny's attention that a servant had just returned to the school after a lengthy absence. Fanny excused herself from the President and spoke some words of encouragement to the servant, and then returned to Mr. Polk. Realizing she may have appeared rude to the President of the United States, she apologized to him.

"You have done well," he said, "I commend you for it. Kindness to those in the humblest capacity of life should be our rule of conduct. By this act you have won not only my respect but my esteem."

9
Fanny's First Book

By 1844, Fanny Crosby had a large number of poems to her credit. Some of these were published in magazines and newspapers, but perhaps a larger portion of them were used for special occasions, such as dedication programs or welcome addresses. Many of Fanny's schoolmates and some of her teachers urged her to gather some of the better ones and publish a book of poetry. Her health was poor during those years, and the task seemed at first too great an undertaking. But when Mr. Hamilton Murray, who was on the school's Board of Managers and a good friend of Fanny's, agreed to help in the selection, she decided to do it.

The book was published by Wiley and Putnam in 1844, under the title of *The Blind Girl and Other Poems*. On the title page is a brief quotation of Milton, a poet who also was blind:

_____ Who best
Bears his mild yoke, they serve him best: his state
Is kingly.

In Mr. Murray's long preface, among other things he stated:

Whatever merit the public may accord to these effusions, most of which were addressed to personal friends as occasioned by the incidents to which they refer, and were not designed for the press; it may rest assured that the several pieces are the unaided productions of the authoress. They were penned from dictation, with very little revision by herself, and less from any other source. Thus in many instances much of the spirit of the composition may have been lost by punctuation, which had it been done by the composer, would convey more justly the thought intended.

With these prefatory remarks, the book is thrown into the prolific tide, which now flows from that vast machine 'the Press,' hardly venturing to hope, that amidst its teeming productions, much pecuniary advantage will be realized to 'The Blind Girl,' for whose benefit it is published, and whose declining health renders its avails the more important.

It is however believed, that a feeling, kindered to that which prompts the writer to the present publication, will influence those to whom it is now offered.

Regarding her "declining health," Fanny Crosby some sixty years later, reflected on Mr. Murray's statement:

"So strange are the decrees of the Master of the Universe! I have outlived my good friend for thirty-five years, and, although then in delicate health, do not consider myself so at the present."

Following the preface is Fanny's own dedication of the book to the Board of Managers:

> Since those whose judgment I esteem
> Superior to my own,
> These scattered thoughts, which have employed
> My leisure hours alone,
> Advise, that to the public eye
> They should presented be:
> Though such a step, till counselled thus,
> Had ne'er occurred to me:
> The course, which author's have pursued,
> I too would imitate,
> And to some valued friend or friends
> This work would dedicate.

Whom should I more revere than those,
Who o'er my youthful hours,
Have long the faithful guardians been.
And strewed my path with flowers?
But language how inadequate
Their kindness to express!
Yet God's all-seeing eye beholds—
And will that kindness bless.
This feeble token of esteem,
Dear friends, to you I bring:
Accept the grateful tribute then—
"Affection's offering."

The first poem in the book is "The Blind Girl," the poem that gave the book its title. It is a long one, filling seven pages in the book. Although the heroine is "Anna," Fanny spoke of the poem being "partly autobiographical." The first few lines say:

Her home was near an ancient wood,
Where many an oak gigantic stood,
And fragrant flowers of every hue
In that sequestered valley grew—

A church there reared its little spire;
And in their neat and plain attire,
The humble peasants would repair
On Sabbath morn, to worship there;

And on the laughing breeze would float
The merry warbler's choral note,
When at Aurora's rosy dawn,
She decked with light the dewy lawn.

A pearly stream meander'd there;
And on its verdant banks so fair,
From school released, at close of day,
A group of happy girls would play.

With their gay laugh the woodlands rang;
Or if some rustic air they sang,

Those rural notes, of music sweet,
Echo, would in mock tones repeat.

Amid those scenes of mirth and glee,
That sightless girl, oh where was she?
Was she, too blithely sporting there,
Or wreathing garlands for her hair?

She sat beside her cottage door;
Her brow a pensive sadness wore;
And while she listened to the song
That issued from that youthful throng;

The tears, warm gushing on her cheek,
Told what no language e'er could speak;
While their young hearts were light and gay,
Her hours passed heavily away.—

A mental night was o'er her thrown;
She sat dejected, and alone.
Yet, no: a mother's accents dear,
Came softly on that blind girl's ear.

While all were locked in dreamy sleep,
That mother, o'er her couch would weep,
And as she knelt in silence there,
Would breathe to God her fervent prayer;
"That He, all merciful and mild,
Would bless her sightless—only child."

The story continues and near the end of the poem it is revealed that Anna is finally enrolled in a school for the blind. The poem concludes:

If o'er the past her memory stray,
Then *music's* sweet and charming lay,
Drives each dark vision from her breast,
And lulls each heaving sigh to rest.
Her grateful lips breathe many a prayer
For him who kindly placed her there.

In the early 1840s, Fanny Crosby wrote for some prestigious magazines, including the *Saturday Emporium* and the *Saturday Evening Post*. Others not so well known were the *Fireman's Journal* and the *Clinton Signal*. Her writing steadily improved and later when Fanny looked back upon the gradual progression of events she could see how it was all a part of God's plan in preparing her for the work to follow.

That great American statesman Henry Clay visited the school in March of 1848. Several months before his visit, his son and namesake had fallen in the battle of Buena Vista. On hearing of the sad event, Fanny composed and mailed to the father the following poem:

> Lo on the blood-stained battlefield,
>   A wounded hero lying;
> Dim is the lustre of his eye,
>   For he, alas! is dying!
>
> See, how with feeble hands he grasps
>   The sword, so faithful ever!
> Now drops the weapon from his side,
>   To be resumed—no never!
>
> O gallant Clay!   though for thy brow
>   Its laurels Fame is weaving,
> Vain trophies these!—thy bosom now
>   Its last faint sigh is heaving.
>
> Back tyrants!—would ye deeper make
>   The wounds already given?
> You, from an aged father's heart,
>   Another tie have riven.
>
> Intrepid warrior!—thou hast left
> A deathless name behind thee:
> That name, unsullied, bright shall shine,
> Though the dark grave may find thee!

Thou by thy General's side hast fought;
And Taylor will deplore thee,
And many a heart that loved thee dear,
Will weep in silence o'er thee.

When the elder Clay visited the Institution, Fanny prepared a welcome address in verse, careful not to mention the mournful event so fresh on his mind and hers. When it came her turn to speak, the blind girl stood and recited:

It comes, it swells, it breaks upon the ear;
Millions have caught the spirit-stirring sound.
And we with joy, with transport uncontrolled,
Would in the chorus of our city join:
Thou noblest of the noble, welcome here!
Noble in high born deeds of spotless fame—
Yes, in behalf of those who o'er us watch,
We bid thee welcome to this lovely spot,
Our peaceful home, where kindred souls are knit
In one sweet bond of friendship unalloyed.
It is not ours thy lineaments to trace,
The intellectual brow, the flashing eye.
Whose glance the language of the soul portrays.
But fancy's busy hand the picture draws,
And with a smile, the glowing sketch presents
To hearts that with anticipation throb.
How have we longed to meet thee, thou whose voice,
In eloquence resistless, like a spell,
Holds e'en a nation captive to its powers!
Well may Columbia of her son be proud.
Firm as a rock, amid conflicting storms,
Thou by her side hast ever fearless stood,
With truth thy motto, principle thy guide.
And thou canst feel as rich a gem is thine,
As ever graced the loftiest monarch's brow:
A nation's honor and a nation's love.
O'er Ashland veiled in winter's cheerless night,
Ere long will steal the gentle breath of spring;
And thou wilt sit among the shades embowered
Of ancient trees, whose giant branches wave
Around the quiet home thou lovest so dear.

The winding streamlet on whose pearly breast
Will murmur on; and when the blushing morn
Calls nature from a soft and dewy sleep
The birds will glad thee with their gushing songs,
So sweetly caroled to the newborn day.
Once more, illustrious statesman, welcome here!
Language can do no more, these trembling lips
To our emotions utterance cannot give.
Yet we would ask, ere thou from us depart,
Oh, let thine accents greet each anxious ear.
Speak, we entreat thee, but one parting word,
That in the secret chambers of the heart
May live the memory of its thrilling tones,
When he who uttered them is far away.

Although Fanny had purposely neglected to mention the death of the statesman's son, the elder Clay had not forgotten the kindness she showed on that occasion. He took her by the arm and led her back to the front of the platform.

"This is not the only poem for which I am indebted to this lady," he said. "Six months ago she sent me some lines on the death of my dear son." His voice wavered and he was unable to speak for a few moments. Fanny wept. When Mr. Clay regained his voice he delivered an address which the blind girl later said was "one of the most eloquent addresses to which I have ever listened."

One of Fanny's early ambitions was to be a teacher—to help educate and encourage others who were blind. S. Trevena Jackson, a minister and close friend of hers quoted her in 1915, as saying:

"I have been interested in schools, teachers, and teaching all my life. A teacher can inspire or depress a pupil. When I was a student some of my teachers did not understand me, and thereby were quite unable to give me what I needed."

Upon her graduation in 1847, Fanny Crosby did not have to wait to realize that ambition of being a teacher. She was immediately retained as a teacher in the New York Institution for the Blind.

10
A Black Cloud Gathers

During the 1840s, reports of the "death blow" started arriving at the New York Institution for the Blind. It was the dread disease of cholera. The beginning of this outbreak was believed to have centered around a town some seventy miles northeast of Calcutta, India. Down through the years and into modern times the malady has remained a major problem in that part of the world, as well as in other parts. It is still considered up to 60 percent fatal if left untreated, and in many cases death occurs in spite of treatment. Available medication in the nineteenth century did little to check the disease and people looked upon an epidemic of it as almost certain death.

The disease moved across Asia and into Europe like prairie fire, and those at the Institution listened for reports of it and wondered if the awesome infection would reach the United States and New York.

At Teheran, Persia, the disease left thousands of people dead in its wake. Many British soldiers were stationed in India at the time and their number was greatly reduced because of it. Cholera would attack an individual with no warning and death often came within a few hours.

The disease thrived in the summer heat, going through Germany and raging into England. When it extended beyond England, some estimates say that seventy thousand people had died since the outbreak.

There was not much that pupils and teachers at the Institution could do except pray and wait. The wait was not long, for a ship landed in New York harbor and on it were several persons who had symptoms of the disease. Within a few days, a number of people died in New York, some of the deaths attributed to cholera. Grim Death had begun his attack in this country.

Attacks came from other areas, too. Soon an emigrant ship landed at the port of New Orleans, the crew having buried seventeen cholera victims at sea prior to arrival. There were no symptoms of the disease among the surviving passengers, and the city of New Orleans breathed a sigh of relief.

Within a few days, though, one woman who had arrived on the ship became ill and was sent to Charity Hospital. It was found she had the infectious disease, and within a few more weeks more than three thousand people died in New Orleans and the surrounding area.

The Mississippi River was in those days one of the chief means of transportation. As it carried passengers, it carried disease. Cholera spread to Memphis, Saint Louis, Cincinnati, Chicago, and eastward.

One morning the superintendent at the Institution rushed into the office and asked Fanny, "Will you promise not to tell what has happened?" She promised and he told her of a man in the neighborhood who had come down with cholera. The sick man was rushed to the hospital on a common cart, the only means of conveyance available at the moment, and died enroute. The students had not yet left the school for their summer vacations, and Fanny knew the danger they faced.

On the following Monday one of the younger girls became ill. The child asked for Fanny and wanted to be held on her lap. When Fanny took the child in her arms, the child said, "Miss Crosby, I am going home, and I just wanted to bid you good-bye and to tell you I love you. Now lay me down again." She died that evening and before sunrise the next morning others at the school carried her body to Trinity Cemetery. A brief prayer was said and as dawn broke the eastern sky, Fanny and the group walked back to the school to watch for new symptoms of the disease.

The school nurse refused to leave her post for vacation and so did Fanny. Fanny acted as a nurse and assisted Dr. J. W. Clements in every way she could. The main remedy was cholera pills, made by hand and consisting of three parts mercury and one part opium. The chore of rolling these ingredients into pills rested for the most part on Fanny, and on one day six hundred of the pills were made.

One evening Fanny felt that she herself had the symptoms of cholera. She excused herself from duty a little earlier that evening, took some of the pills and retired for the night. On awaking she found the symptoms were gone, and she praised the Lord for it.

As the disease neared its peak, memories were being made that would remain with Fanny as long as she lived. On one occasion, when she was making her way from looking in on a patient in one room to a patient in another across the hall, she stumbled on a casket in the hallway. Night after night she heard carts grinding their way up and down the streets and the hoarse cry of the drivers, "Bring out your dead!"

Finally, the doctor and superintendent ordered Fanny to go home for a rest. The surviving twenty students who had remained at the school during the vacation were transferred to Whitlockville, New York.

That fall the mayor of New York City sent out a letter via the news media urging the people to return to their homes. The epidemic was subsiding in New York and the nation after taking a huge toll of lives.

> In Thy cleft, O Rock of Ages,
> Hide Thou me;
> When the fitful temptest rages,
> Hide Thou me;
> Where no mortal arm can sever
> From my heart Thy love forever,
> Hide me O Thou Rock of Ages, Safe in Thee.

From the snare of sinful pleasure,
Hide Thou me;
Thou my soul's eternal treasure,
Hide Thou me;
When the world its power is wielding,
And my heart is almost yielding,
Hide me, O Thou Rock of Ages, Safe in Thee.

In the lonely night of sorrow,
Hide Thou me;
Till in glory dawns the morrow,
Hide Thou me;
In the sight of Jordan's billow,
Let Thy bosom be my pillow;
Hide me, O Thou Rock of Ages, Safe in Thee.

11
Fanny Blushes

Winfield Scott was a hero in the War of 1812. In the Mexican War he became a famous American general, performing an important role in the capture of Mexico City in 1847. Later in 1848, he visited New York City and the New York Institution for the Blind.

Mr. Chamberlain, superintendent of the school, gave the welcome address, a speech Fanny Crosby called "a model of his excellent use of the English tongue." In his closing remarks, Mr. Chamberlain said:

> Some of these pupils, when you have filled up the measure of your fame, and to you, the praise and censure of men will be alike indifferent,—they will survive; and when they shall recount your achievements, and tell to coming generations of Chippewa, and of Cerro Gordo, and of Contreras, and many other fields where you have covered the proud flag of your country with imperishable glory,—I would have them say, too, that once at least it was their fortune to listen to the tones of that voice, whose word of command was ever to the brave the tailsman of assured victory.

General Scott gave his brief but sincere reply and when he had finished, Fanny asked him, "General Scott, when you found yourself really within the halls of the Montezumas, did you not feel like shouting?"

"No," he replied, "we felt like falling down on our knees to thank the good Lord for our victory."

Later in the afternoon when the General was examining some maps used by the blind students, someone noticed his sword was out of place and looked as if it would fall on the floor. This was mentioned to Fanny, and she crept to his side, lifted the sword and held it over his head.

"General Scott," she exclaimed in a military manner, "you are my prisoner!"

General Scott was taken by surprise but, as usual, he had a ready answer.

"Oh, I surrender; I always surrender at discretion to the ladies," and he, Fanny, and those who observed the incident enjoyed a hearty laugh.

General Scott, a Whig in politics, was at the time a candidate for the office of President of the United States, but to Fanny's embarrassment, she momentarily forgot that fact when he made the statement, "Well, Miss Crosby, the next time I come here I suppose some young man will have run off with you."

"Oh, no," she answered, "I shall wait for the next president." A roar of laughter came from those who overheard the remark, and Fanny blushed when she realized why they were amused.

Winfield Scott, however, was not nearly so successful in his bid for the presidency as he was in his campaign for Mexico City. Franklin Pierce, another general, won the election.

Fanny Crosby was quite interested in politics and the government of her country in general, and her writing talent provided her with an active role in the political campaigns. She composed many slogans and songs for the candidates, one of which stated:

> O Whigs, carry me on, carry me far away,
> For election's past
> And I'm *Pierced* at last:
> The *locoes* have gained the day.

As one might infer from those lines, Fanny's favorite candidate in that election was the Democrat, Franklin Pierce, who won over the Whig, Winfield Scott, and the candidate of the Free Soil Party, John Parker Hale. Pierce received 1,601,274 votes; Scott received 1,386,580; and Hale, 155,825.

On the other hand, Fanny's political remarks sometimes placed her in uncomfortable positions. A few years previous to the campaign just mentioned, the Democrat candidates were James K. Polk and George Mifflin, and the Whig candidates were Henry Clay and Theodore Frelinghuysen. Fanny Crosby was seated one day in the parlor and for her own amusement was singing some of her political songs. When she finished, someone approached her and said, "Then Mr. Clay is not your candidate."

"No," she replied, "but I have profound respect and reverence for him, and also for Mr. Frelinghuysen, yet they are not my candidates." Just then Mr. Chamberlain came up and introduced Fanny and the man who had just spoken to her. To Fanny's amazement it was Theodore Frelinghuysen himself!

"Mr. Frelinghuysen," she said, "you have heard me express my views already, and for me to say that I did not mean it would be telling a falsehood. But I would have not said what I did, had I known you were present, so please take it for what it is worth."

Mr. Frelinghuysen laughed and said, "I give you credit for your candor."

Throughout Fanny's life she was patriotic and interested in the affairs of her country. As recent as 1906, she stated:

My interest in public affairs has never abated. There are not many people living in this year of grace who had the privilege of meeting such statesmen as Henry Clay, General Scott, and President Polk; but the names of these heroes are recorded with indelible letters among the annals of our national history and their imperishable deeds are chronicled in the characters that no person living should wish to efface. They were men of sterling worth and firm integrity, of whom the rising generation may well learn wisdom and the true principles of national honor and democracy that all of them labored so faithfully to inculcate. And that the men of this present age and of generations to come will continue to remember the dignity and honor that the past has bequeathed to our own and future times, no loyal American need have one iota of doubt.

Visitors to the school were not limited to men in government. Others were men and women in the musical, entertainment, and literary fields. One of these that came in the early 1840s was William Cullen Bryant, the American poet. How thrilled Fanny Crosby was when she heard of his planned visit! She said:

> As was the case almost wherever he went, he was obliged to hold a little impromptu reception at our soiree; and among those that were introduced to him, was poor little timid I, who had very little hope that he would greet me otherwise than conventionally, and as a stranger of whom he had never heard before.
>
> To my surprise, however, he gave me a warm grasp of the hand, commented upon my poor little rhythmical efforts, commended them in a tone that I felt to be sincere, and told me to go on bravely and determinedly with my work. He never knew how much good he did, by those few words, to the young girl that had hardly hoped to touch the hem of his proud robe of poetic genius!

Horace Greeley, an outspoken man in many social reforms and founder of the New York *Tribune,* visited the school in 1844. Fanny commented:

> But I must say, that I at first was disappointed in him: perhaps I expected too much. "Is *that* the great Horace Greeley?" I pondered, after hearing him talk. I had never

been able to read any of his editorials, but concluded, in my inexperience, that if they were no more brilliant than his conversation, the world was making a queer mistake in honoring him.

The following summer I happened to meet him at the house of a mutual friend; and a more charming and intelligent conversationalist, I never heard. History, literature, social ethics, political economy—all subjects—seemed perfectly natural and easy to him; and no one else wished to talk, so long as he could be kept talking.

Of course, being human, I did not admire him one whit the less, when he insisted on my reciting to him some of my little poems, praised them, and invited me to write for his paper!

And, of course, Fanny did write for the New York *Tribune*, as well as other great papers and magazines of the day.

Ole Bull, the Norwegian violinist, was born in 1810 and was thus ten years older than Fanny. He toured Europe and America playing beautiful violin music—mostly his own compositions. He, too, visited the Institution, and Fanny Crosby later said of his visit:

Having heard a great deal about his wonderful playing on the violin, I, like other girls, was wild to hear him play. When it was announced that Ole Bull was to pay us a visit, you can just imagine how I felt. I can weep over it even now. It seemed as I literally *saw* him, as he drew his bow over the strings of his violin. The birds sang, the brooks rippled, the rain fell, the thunder roared, the sunbeams danced, the bells pealed, the angels sang. We were all enchanted. Burning tears of joy coursed down my cheeks and a light celestial threw its halo over my brow. When I grasped the hand of Ole Bull I felt as if I were touching one from another world. We sat down together. He talked with me and his words charmed and cheered me.

Martin F. Tupper, an English poet, also visited the school. And however good his talent for writing poetry may have been, his ability to speak in public evidently was not so good. One of his poems states:

> Never give up, it is wiser and better
> Always to hope than once to despair,
> Throw off the yoke with its conquering fetter,
> Yield not a moment to sorrow or care.
> Never give up, though adversity presses,
> Providence wisely has mingled the cup;
> And the best counsel in all our distresses
> Is the stout watchword, Never give up.

In his attempt to recite the poem on his visit to the Institution, Mr. Tupper became confused when he reached the third line. Fanny, sitting behind him and familiar with the poem, prompted him. He continued and when he reached the third line of the second stanza, his memory again failed him. Fanny again prompted him, but instead of going on he said, "It is of no use; this lady knows my poem better than I do; and therefore I will sit down." And in apparent violation of the advice in his poem, Poet Tupper gave up.

Alice Cary, a poet and sister of Phoebe Cary, who was also a poet, visited the school. She was the same age as Fanny and the two became permanent friends.

Jenny Lind, the singer known as "The Swedish Nightingale," was a guest at the school in 1850, and her golden voice charmed teachers and students alike. Fanny Crosby welcomed her with the following original lines:

> We ask no more why strains like thine,
> Enchant a listening throng,
> For we have felt in one sweet hour
> The magic of thy song.
>
> How like the carol of a bird,
> It stole upon my ear!

Then tenderly it died away
In echoes soft and clear.

But hark! again its music breaks
Harmonious on the soul:
How thrills the heart, at every tone,
With bliss beyond control!

If strains like these, so pure and sweet,
To mortal lips be given,
What must the glorious anthems be
Which angels wake in heaven?

'Tis past; 'tis gone. That fairy dream
Of happiness is o'er;
And we the music of thy voice
Perhaps may hear no more.

Yet, Sweden's daughter, thou shalt live
In every grateful heart;
And may the choicest gifts of heaven
Be thine, where'er thou art.

Other singers who came and with whom Fanny became acquainted were Adeline Patti, Clara Louise Kellogg, and Madam LeGrange. The latter burst into tears during one of her numbers, because of her sympathy for the blind students.

Fanny Crosby's first book had been well received, and in 1851, she was urged to assemble poems for a second volume. She did so and it was published that year under the title *Monterey and Other Poems*.

The second book, like the first, quoted Milton on its title page:

As the wakeful bird
Sings darkling, and in shadiest covert hid
Tunes her nocturnal note.

Fanny was frequently ill during those months and she mentioned her poor health in the last paragraph of the preface:

With health sadly impaired, and a consequent frequent inability to discharge those duties from which I have hitherto derived a maintenance, the pecuniary emolument there may arise from the sale of the work, will be acceptable as it will be appreciated; and the Blind Girl's declining years be thereby rendered unclouded by that dependency so repulsive to a mind ever active, and a hand, when not enervated by disease, ever assiduous for her self-support.

In spite of that statement and the condition of her health at that time, her physical condition improved and she lived nearly sixty-four additional years, in good health!

The book contains more than two hundred pages of poetry, and one poem near the end of the book is called "The Wish":

> I ask; but not the glittering pomp
> Of wealth and pageantry;
> Nor splendid dome; a rural cot
> My domicile shall be.
>
> 'Tis not to mingle with the gay,
> The opulent, and proud;
> 'Tis not to court the flattering smile
> Of an admiring crowd.
>
> I ask a heart—a faithful heart—
> Congenial with mine own,
> Whose deep, unchanging love shall burn
> For me, and me alone.
>
> A heart in sorrow's cheerless hour,
> To soften every care;
> To taste with me the sweets of life,
> And all its ills to share.
>
> Thus linked by friendship's golden chain,
> Ah! who more blessed than we;
> Unruffled as the pearly stream,
> Our halcyon days would be.

Fanny and some of the other teachers and students often attended services at the Eighteenth Street Methodist Church, and on Thursday evenings a leader from the church came to the Institution to teach a class.

"I must confess," Fanny said, "that I had grown somewhat indifferent to the means of grace, so much so, in fact, that I attended the meetings and played for them on the condition that they should not call on me to speak."

One Thursday evening, Theodore Camp came to the school with the leader from the church. Mr. Camp was a teacher in the public schools and known for his general public spirit. He was placed in charge of the industrial department of the Institution in 1845, and he and Fanny became friends. She often consulted him in matters of importance and followed his advice.

One night Fanny dreamed she found Mr. Camp very ill and near death. The conversation in the dream was as follows:

"Fanny, can you give up our friendship?"

"No, I cannot; you have been my advisor and friend and what could I do without your aid?"

"But, why would you chain a spirit to earth when it longs to fly away and be at rest?" Mr. Camp asked.

"Well," she answered, "I cannot give you up of myself but I will seek Divine assistance."

"But will you meet me in Heaven?"

"Yes, I will, God helping me," she replied.

"Remember your promise to a dying man," he said and Fanny awoke.

The remarks in that dream came to Fanny's mind often during the next several months.

Later in the autumn of 1850, a series of revival meetings was in progress at the Thirtieth Street Methodist Church. Fanny and others of her group attended these services. As the meetings progressed, Fanny Crosby realized something was lacking in her life. She felt empty and incomplete.

The auditorium was huge and to the blind girl sitting near the center, it must have seemed larger than it was. On two occasions someone went with her to the altar and prayed with her, but each time she came away without the assurance she longed for.

The series of meetings was rapidly drawing to a close. On the night of November 20, 1850, when the altar call was given, Fanny slipped quietly away from her friends and made her way alone down the long aisle to the altar. It seemed to her that the light must come then or never.

After a prayer was offered, the congregation started singing a hymn written by Isaac Watts and Ralph E. Hudson,

> Alas, and did my Saviour bleed,
> And did my Sovereign die?
> Would He devote that sacred head
> For such a worm as I?

And when they sang the line "Here Lord, I give myself away," Fanny Crosby realized that she had been trying to hold onto the world with one hand and hold onto God with the other. She let go of the world and rose to her feet, shouting the victory!

12
Popular Songs

One of the most successful writers of popular music during the last century was George F. Root, who was born in Sheffield, Massachusetts, on August 30, 1820, and died on August 6, 1895.

Mr. Root composed such favorites as "Battle Cry of Freedom," "Tramp, Tramp, Tramp," "Just Before the Battle, Mother," and "There's Music in the Air." What was not and still is not commonly known is that the lyrics to these familiar songs were not all written by Mr. Root. The words for "There's Music in the Air," for example, were written by none other than Fanny Crosby, the blind lady who was later to become the world's most prolific writer of hymns.

What his motive was for omitting her by-line from these compositions is not known. Apparently, though, it was that he simply didn't put much emphasis on by-lines, for he never attempted otherwise to conceal the information. In fact, in his autobiography *The Story of a Musical Life*, published in 1891, he expressed his indebtedness to Miss Crosby:

At the Institution for the Blind there was at that time a lady who had been a pupil there, but was now a teacher, who had a great gift of rhyming, and, better still, had a delicate and poetic imagination. The name of Fanny Crosby was not known then beyond the small circle of her personal friends, but it is now familiar, especially wherever gospel songs are sung. I used to tell her one day in prose what I wanted the Flowers or Recluse to say, and the next day the poem would be ready—sometimes two or three of them. I generally hummed enough of a melody to give her an idea of the meter and rhythmic swing wanted, and sometimes played to her the entire music of a number before she undertook her work. It was all the same. Like many blind people her memory was great, and she easily retained all I told her. After receiving her poems, which rarely needed any modification, I thought out the music, perhaps while going from one lesson to another, and then I caught the first moment of freedom to write it out. This went on until the cantata was finished.

When George Root was six the family moved to North Reading, Massachusetts. In 1838, at the age of eighteen, he went to Boston to study with a musician by the name of A. N. Johnson. Not long afterward he became Mr. Johnson's teaching assistant and also served as organist at the Winter Street and Park Street Churches. In Boston he also met Lowell Mason, a writer of sacred and other types of music. Mr. Root helped him in his work at the Boston Academy of Music.

Mr. Root moved to New York in 1844, and became singing teacher at Abbott's School, a school for girls. He also became organist at the Mercer Street Presbyterian Church. A little later he began teaching classes at three additional schools: Rutgers Female Institute, Miss Haine's school for young ladies, and Union Theological Seminary.

In 1845 George F. Root married Mary Olive Woodman, a singer of popular songs and the sister of J. G. Woodman, an organist and composer. And it was in that same year that he began giving musical instruction at the New York Institution for the Blind. One day he played an air that Fanny Crosby described as "wonderfully sweet and touching."

"Oh, Mr. Root," she said, "why don't you publish that?"

"I have no words for it," he replied, "and cannot purchase any." Fanny asked for and received permission to attempt the job herself. She wrote:

O come to the greenwood, where nature is smiling,
Come to the greenwood, so lovely and gay,
There will soft music thy spirit beguiling
Tenderly carol thy sadness away.

Another joint composition by Fanny Crosby and George F. Root was a song about a black man saddened by the death of his sweetheart, called "Fare Thee Well, Kitty Dear." The chorus of it states:

Fare thee well, Kitty dear,
Thou art sleeping in thy grave so low,
Nevermore, Kitty dear,
Wilt thou listen to my old banjo.

During the late 1840s and early 1850s Fanny and George Root collaborated to produce fifty or sixty songs that met with overwhelming success. Among these were "Bird of the North," "Hazel Dell," "They Have Sold Me Down the River," "O How Glad to Get Home," "Rosalie the Prairie Flower," "Proud World, Good-bye," "The Honeysuckle Glen," "All Together," "Never Forget the Dear Ones," and, as was mentioned at the beginning of this chapter, "There's Music in the Air." Royalty from "Rosalie the Prairie Flower" alone amounted to nearly three thousand dollars, a rather large sum especially in those days.

Around mid-century, William B. Bradbury was presenting some floral concerts at the Broadway Tabernacle. This gave Mr. Root the idea to compose a cantata for use in his classes, particularly those at Rutgers and Springler Institute. He picked the subject of a flower choosing a queen. He prepared the music and Fanny Crosby the words to their first cantata, and they named their new creation *The Flower Queen*. The story in the play was of an old man who had become tired of the world and decided to become a hermit. But as he was about to retire to his lonely dwelling he heard a chorus singing, "Who shall be queen of the flowers?" His interest was aroused and on the following day he was asked to judge in a contest where each flower presented her claims of why she should be queen of all the others. Finally, the would-be-hermit chose the rose for her loveliness, and in turn the rose urged him to return to the world and his duty.

Other cantatas thus produced were *Daniel* and *The Pilgrim Fathers,* the music for the latter written jointly by George Root and Lowell Mason.

The words to some of the popular songs that Fanny wrote are published in another chapter of this book. For example, "Rosalie the Prairie Flower" was perhaps her most successful one and is given in that chapter, as is her most enduring one, "There's Music in the Air." A close runner-up is "The Honeysuckle Glen," and it is given here:

In the honeysuckle glen, where odors sweet
Perfume the breeze that floats along,
And the rosy tints of morn with blushes greet
The lark as she trills her song;
In the honeysuckle glen, how pleasantly
The happy summer days would glide,
When I wandered by the rill, so merrily,
And Lilla was by my side.

In the honeysuckle glen, secluded far,
The home of nature's fairest bowers,
When with mild and gentle light the evening star
Looks forth on the dewy flowers;
In the honeysuckle glen, how tenderly
I looked upon my lovely bride,
And I never dreamed that care could reach me there
When Lilla was by my side

Through the honeysuckle glen I've wandered now
For many weary years alone;
O, I never more shall see her angel brow,
Or list to her winning tone;
But the parting words she spoke I cherish still,
And wear them on my breaking heart,
Till I meet her on that shore, our sorrows o'er,
Where loved ones no more shall part.

Chorus: Lilla, Lilla, wake again
From thy sleep in the honeysuckle glen;
Lilla, dearest, all is o'er,
Thou wilt return no more.

13
Pranks and Humor

When gathering material for this book I interviewed a number of people. Some are related to Fanny Crosby, and others were acquainted with her during her final years. There is a lady in Bridgeport, Connecticut and one in Sacramento, California, who actually remember seeing Fanny and talking with her. Both of these ladies remarked about Fanny Crosby's amazing sense of humor. She enjoyed a hearty laugh.

Although Fanny was in her mid-eighties when she wrote the story of her life, she recalled many things that happened to her during her lifetime and which still caused her to chuckle, even at that advanced age.

During her school days her reputation as a prankster was so well known that when something was amiss she often would get the blame for it even when she was innocent. "That looks like another of Fanny's tricks," someone would say.

The New York Institution for the Blind in those days grew an annual vegetable garden to defray the food expense. One year a fine crop of watermelons was included in the garden. When the melons were almost ready for harvesting, a rumor was circulated that the melons were to be sold for the benefit of the school. The students voiced, and perhaps exaggerated, their disappointment that they were not to be permitted to eat the delicious fruit they worked so hard to produce.

Fanny Crosby, then eighteen years old, and a few of her classmates decided they would do something to alter the situation: they would have at least one of those juicy melons!

Late that night, Fanny took one of the smaller girls and slipped into the garden. Fanny gave the girl the instructions and almost immediately heard footsteps. She quickly hid the smaller girl as Mr. Stevens, the gardener, approached.

"Why, Mr. Stevens!" she exclaimed. "Are you here? How do you happen to be walking up and down at this hour of the night?"

"I'm watching out for some of them miserable boys that's tryin' to steal the melons," he said. "I'll catch them yet!"

"Don't you want me to watch awhile for you, Mr. Stevens?" she asked the old man as nonchalantly as she could. "You go and sit down for fifteen minutes, and I'll stay out here and watch for you. And depend upon it, if a single boy comes, I'll let you know."

She led the old gentleman indoors, sat him down, and coaxed him into relaxing, while she watched the garden. She then returned to the garden and told the girl to carry the selected melon to their room. After about fifteen minutes, she went again to Mr. Stevens and told him that "not a boy has been by." She then returned to her room, where she and the others enjoyed their prized possession. Years later, Fanny told the superintendent of the incident and both enjoyed an exuberant laugh.

The school often had visitors, ranging from public officials who would come to check on the school's progress, to just plain curious individuals. Some of the students resented continually being put on public display and answering the same questions again and again.

One boy was guiding a group of ladies on a tour of the school and when they came to the dining hall, one of the women asked how blind people manage to find the way to their mouths without slopping food on themselves.

"We hitch one end of a string to the leg of our chair and the other end to our tongue and just follow the string," the weary boy replied.

Fanny loved to relate humorous incidents or jokes about ministers. A favorite one was also a true one about a minister who was talking on the subject of stewardship, when one man protested, "But the dying thief was converted and went direct to heaven, and he never gave anything towards the heathen nor the expenses of the church!"

"No," the minister replied, "but he was a *dying* thief, and you are a *living* thief!"

On the same subject, Fanny told the following story:

A young minister friend of mine once went up to a quiet New England town to spend his vacation with his little boy. The father had given close attention to the training of his only son. They were really companions. The mother had been taken to the Better Land when the boy was born. The preacher had not been in town a week before a deacon of the church came and requested him to preach on Sunday morning, as the man engaged had disappointed them. After some talk with the farmer-deacon the minister consented . . . . The service ended without an offering being taken, and it had been the custom of this minister never to appear in the sanctuary without bringing an offering to the Lord. So as he left the church he placed a fifty-cent piece in the box by the door and went down the winding "Pine Path." In a few seconds he heard a voice and turning he saw the deacon hastening towards him, who placed in his hand a fifty-cent piece, saying, "It is our custom up here to present the preacher with whatever we find in the offering boxes for his services." Then the minister's little boy looked up into his father's face and said, "Papa, if you had given more you would have gotten more, wouldn't you?"

Fanny enjoyed teasing a postman who delivered mail to the Institution. She would often hide his letter book or the pen and ink. One day when it was raining heavily, she put her verse-making talent to work and scribbled a message and left it on the desk for him to find:

> Postman, come not yet,
> Wait till the storm is past,
> Or you'll a ducking get;
> The rain is falling fast.

You have a new white hat,
As I have heard them say;
Then, postman, think of that!
Don't venture out today!

Presumptuous man, in vain
To stay your course I sing;
In spite of wind or rain
The letters you will bring;
Though you are such a dunce
I will not cruel be,
But ask our nurse at once
To make some flax-seed tea.

From early school days, Fanny Crosby and Alice Holmes, who also was a poet, were permanent friends. When Alice first moved into Fanny's room at the school, Fanny found that Alice was a member of the Episcopal Church, while Fanny was an adherent of the Methodist. Fanny told her to listen to a verse she had written and to appraise it. She recited to Alice:

Oh, how it grieves my poor old bones,
To sleep so near that Alice Holmes,
I will inform good Mr. Jones,
I can't sleep with a churchman.

Sometimes the tables were turned to even the score with Fanny. On one such occasion, Fanny had returned to the school from a lecture late one evening and the superintendent spoke to her as she was on the way to her room. He informed her that there was a "Bridgeport Farmer" in the house, who had come to visit her. Thinking one of her friends had arrived in her absence, she retired joyfully and with expectation. The following morning she was up early, and after carefully dressing for the occasion, she walked sprightly down the stairs. The superintendent met her, saying, "Meet your visitor," and he handed her a copy of the *Bridgeport Farmer*, a paper published in Bridgeport, Connecticut.

Although Fanny graduated and became a teacher in the

New York Institution for the Blind, her humor-in-verse did
not end with her graduation. In 1850, she wrote a poem based
on an actual incident between a mouse and a "Mr. C." It may
have been Mr. J. F. Chamberlain, who was superintendent of
the Institution from 1846 to 1852.

The Presumptuous Mouse

Dear friends, receive attentively
A strange account of Mr. C.
With your permission I'll relate,—
Though you may smile at his sad fate,—
How while reposing on his bed,
And airy thoughts flit through his head,
A weary mouse house-hunting crept,
Close to the pillow where he slept;
But there not feeling quite at ease,
And wishing much himself to please,
He looked with grave and thoughtful air
On Mr. C's dishevelled hair.
"Ah, here's the station I like best,"
Said he, "and here I'll build my nest.
This scalp conceals a poet's brain,
So here till morning I'll remain,
Perhaps the muse will me inspire,
And if she tune her magic lyre,
I'll to the world proclaim that we,
That mice, like men, may poets be."
Our hero thus descanted long
On love, and poesy and song;
While now and then a gentle squeal
His vocal powers would reveal.
His strain of eloquence it broke,
For Mr. C, perplexed awoke,
And starting up—"I do declare
There's something scraping in my hair;
A light; a light; what shall I do?"
At this the mouse, alarmed, withdrew;
And had he not, I'm certain, death
Had stopped, ere long, his little breath.

14
A Secretary Who Became Famous

In the year 1852, Mr. T. Golden Cooper succeeded Mr. Chamberlain as superintendent of the New York Institution for the Blind. Mr. William Cleveland was the principal. In the fall of 1853, Mr. Cleveland took a short leave to attend the funeral of his father, who died on October 1. When he returned to the school he called Fanny Crosby into his office.

"I have a favor to ask of you. My brother, as you may know, has been appointed secretary to the superintendent. But the death of our father grieves him very much. When you are at leisure I wish you would speak to him and try to divert his mind from sad thoughts. You can comfort him better than I can."

Fanny promised to do what she could. That afternoon when she went into the superintendent's office, she found a young man of nearly seventeen years, by the name of Grover Cleveland. Fanny later wrote of that first meeting:

We talked together unreservedly about his father's death, and a bond of friendship sprung up between us, which was strengthened by subsequent interviews. He seemed a very gentle, but intensely ambitious boy, and I felt that there were great things in store for him—although there was no thought in my mind that he would ever be chosen from among the millions of this country, to be its President.

Whether the death of his father had settled his mind into a serious view, or whether it was because industry and perseverance were natural to him, I do not know: but think each of these influences bore a part toward directing his actions.

He very seldom went out to a party or entertainment with others of the same age; but remained in his room, working away at his books. I am told that during his entire career, this faculty of hard and almost incessant work, has been one of his most valuable aids.

Among other very pleasant characteristics which I noticed in him, was a disposition to help others, whenever possible. Knowing that it was a great favor to me to have my poems copied neatly and legibly, he offered to perform that service for me: and I several times availed myself of his aid.

Fanny Crosby and Grover Cleveland, however, failed to consider the view that the superintendent might take of this arrangement. Although Fanny and Grover never neglected their teaching and secretarial duties (he also acted as an assistant teacher) and spent much of their own time in the evenings reading or reciting to the blind students, the superintendent did not look kindly on anyone who did anything without his express permission. In *McClure's Magazine*, April 1909, Fanny is reported as having said: "He [Grover] was always kindly and sympathetic, and during his residence there the tendency was strongly developed at every turn. He resented occasional cruelties practiced by a superintendent who lacked the qualities necessary for a successful administration of such an important place."

Fanny went on to describe how a young boy had been unduly and severely punished, and how young Grover Cleveland had sympathized with the lad but was unable to do much about it, since he was employed as secretary to the one who had administered the punishment. So, when the superintendent came into the room one day and caught Fanny dictating a poem to his secretary, it displeased him greatly.

"I'll have you understand the clerks in this office have other work to do, than to copy poetry," he said and hurried from the office.

Grover, or "Grove" as Fanny called him during those days, laughed and then said, "How long are you going to let that man trample on you feelings in this manner?"

"What shall I do?" Fanny asked.

"You are certainly within your own rights," Grover told her. "So, if you have a poem to be copied tomorrow, come down here, and exactly the same scene will occur as has occurred today. Then, you will have an opportunity to give him as good as he sends; and if you have never learned the lesson of self-reliance, you certainly cannot learn it earlier."

"Why, Grove," Fanny said, "I have never been saucy in my life!"

"But it isn't impudent to take your own part," young Grover Cleveland said.

After thinking about the idea for a few moments, Fanny decided the plan that Grover proposed might be a favor to all concerned: to the school, to the other teachers, to the pupils, to herself and Grover, and possibly to the superintendent himself.

The next day Fanny arrived at Grover's desk on schedule, with some copying to be done—and a little speech for the superintendent. And as predicted, the superintendent came in and started another lecture, but at his first pause, Fanny interjected, "I want you to understand that I am second to no one in this Institution except youself, and I have borne with your insolence so long that I will do so no longer; if it is repeated, I will report you to the Board of Managers."

The superintendent looked at her with great astonishment, and for once he was at a loss for words. As Grover Cleveland had promised, the superintendent's respect for the two grew and his attitude toward others in the school seemed to improve.

Grover remained at the school for a year and then moved on to other work and further education, and eventually, of course, twice became president of the United States. Ter-

minating his tour of duty at the school, however, did not end
their friendship. Grover and Fanny often corresponded, but
Fanny was reluctant to do so while he was in the White
House. She felt to do so she would be imposing upon his
generous nature, and she preferred not to take even a few
minutes from a man whose time was so valuable.

Many years later, in 1891, Fanny visited Mr. and Mrs.
Cleveland in Lakewood, New Jersey. It was soon after their
daughter Ruth was born and Fanny wrote:

Like the lily bells that blossom
In the bowers of Eden fair,
All their pretty leaves unfolding
To the breeze that murmurs there,
Like a jewel bright and sparkling
From the peerless brow of Truth,
Like a birdling with the autumn,
Came your winsome Baby Ruth.

There are feelings deep and tender,
There are joys you could not know
Till a cherub in your household
Bade the hidden fountains flow.
Now, a love its smile reflecting
From the peaceful eye of Truth,
Like a radiant star is shining
O'er your gentle Baby Ruth

In a fancied dream I linger,
As the evening time draws nigh,
And I listen to the carol
Of her mamma's lullaby,
While her papa, grave and thoughtful,
As in years of vanished youth,
Lays his hand with fond caressing
On the head of Baby Ruth.

By a holy consecration
That will ne'er forgotten be,
You have answered Him who whispered
'Bring your little ones to me.'

You have brought her, pure and lovely,
To the Way, the Life, the Truth,
And His seal is on the forehead
Of your precious Baby Ruth.

May you train her in the knowledge
And the wisdom of the Lord,
May you teach her to be faithful,
And obedient to His word.
With the lamp, whose beams are kindled
At the throne of sacred truth,
May you guide the coming future
Of your darling Baby Ruth.

In March, 1903, a man who knew Fanny Crosby only
slightly, wrote to ex-President Grover Cleveland and re-
minded him that on March 24 Fanny would be celebrating
her birthday. He told Mr. Cleveland that if he would send
him a letter addressed to Fanny, he would deliver it to her.
When the letter arrived, instead of delivering it to the blind
lady, he sold it to a reporter and it was published in a newspaper. When Mr. Cleveland learned of the incident, he sent
another letter directly to Fanny, saying:

As an old friend, it is a great pleasure to congratulate you
on your coming birthday, which marks so many years of
usefulness and duty. I am rejoiced to know that your
character and work are amply appreciated by good, kind
friends, who stand about you in your advancing years to
cheer and comfort you. I remember our association fifty
years ago; and it gratifies me to say that you, who have
brought cheer and comfort to so many in the past, richly
deserve now the greatest amount of grateful acknowledgement, and all the rich recompense, which the love of
friends and the approval of God can supply.

Two years later, on Fanny Crosby's eighty-fifth birthday,
Mr. Cleveland mailed her another letter. A copy of this one is

printed in another chapter, under the heading "Fanny's Scrapbook."

Fanny was saddened at the news of the death of Ruth Cleveland, on January 7, 1904, a few months after the child's twelfth birthday. A few years later, on June 24, 1908, Grover himself died. The following day a reporter from the Bridgeport *Telegram* interviewed Fanny. In a two-column story Fanny was quoted as saying, "Oh, yes, they told me today that he was dead. It almost broke my heart. It seems to me that I cannot give him up. Yes, I can give him up, for I have learned to know 'Thy will be done.' "

The blind hymn writer was then asked of the impression Mr. Cleveland had left on her mind. "Impression! He left an impression that will never be effaced—that of a noble, faithful Christian gentleman, and with that impression there was that deep, warm, friendship that death cannot break, for the cords will be united, and we shall see and know each other in the land of the blest."

When the newspaper reporter left, Fanny returned to her work of writing an article a magazine editor had asked for. She knew that if she kept busy she would have little time to think of the sad parting of her old friend, Grover Cleveland. She preferred to remember their days at the Institution and to look forward to the day when they would meet again.

> No sorrow there in yonder clime,
> Beyond the troubled waves of time;
> No dreary nights nor weeping eyes,
> No aching hearts, nor broken ties.
>
> Oh perfect rest, O calm repose,
> Where life's clear stream in beauty flows!
> And we can sing, without a care,
> No sorrow there, no sorrow there.
>
> A little while our watch to keep,
> A little while to wake and sleep,
> To bear the cross, endure the pain—
> And then with Christ forever reign.

15
Wedding Bells

When the group of pupils and teachers from the New York Institution for the Blind made the trip on the Erie Canal, as described in a previous chapter, a lady approached Fanny Crosby and informed her that her son was to be enrolled in the school. She asked Fanny to keep an eye on him and see that no harm came to him, and Fanny agreed to do so.

The young man's name was Alexander Van Alstyne, the son of Wells Van Alstyne, an engineer. The father had come to this country from the banks of the Rhine and had performed an important part in the construction of the Welland Canal.

When Alexander Van Alstyne entered the Institution in 1844, Fanny Crosby had already begun teaching there and had him in some of her classes. She described the young man as a talented musician whose main educational interest lay in the area of music. In 1848, he graduated and went to Union College, in Schenectady, New York. There he studied Greek, Latin, and theology, enriching his life for a musical career. After his graduation from that college, he returned to the New York Institution for the Blind to teach.

The two teachers, Fanny and Alexander, were in close association and became interested in one another. Fanny later wrote of the relationship:

> He was fond of classic literature and theological lore, but made music a specialty. After hearing several of my poems he became deeply interested in my work; and I after listening to his sweet strains of music became interested in him. Thus we soon grew to be very much concerned for each

other. One day in June he went out under the elm trees to
listen to the birds sing, and the winds play their love-song
among the leaves. It was here the voice of love spoke within
his breast. Listening, he heard its voice of music trilling its
notes to his heart. Just then another to whom the voice was
calling came towards the spot where he was musing. I
placed my right hand on his left and called him "Van." Then
it was that two happy lovers sat in silence, while sunbeams
danced around their heads, and the golden curtains of day
drew in their light. "Van" took up the harp of love, and
drawing his fingers over the golden chords, sang to me the
song of a true lover's heart. From that hour two lives looked
on a new universe, for love met love, and all the world was
changed. We were no longer blind, for the light of love
showed us where the lilies bloomed, and where the crystal
waters find the moss-mantled spring.

On March 3, 1858, Fanny Crosby resigned her teaching
position at the Institution for the Blind and two days later she
and Alexander Van Alstyne were united in marriage.

"We found in each other not only perfect congeniality, but
sympathy in our pursuits," Fanny Crosby said. "Neither of us
interfered with the other's professional career. Each of us (as
is not always the case) could sympathize with the other's
occupation, without rivalry or interference. He set several of
my hymns to music: but his taste was mostly for the wordless
melodies of the classics. He insisted that my literary name
should remain as it was: I yielded to his desire, and although
really Mrs. Van Alstyne, have always written under the name
of Fanny Crosby, except when using soubriquets."

Later in her career of hymn writing, when her output
neared its peak, some of her hymns were published under her
married name, as well as many noms de plume. This idea
apparently was that of her publishers, to make it appear to the
public that not all the hymns came from one writer.

Fanny further said of her husband:

He was not only a musician, but a philosopher, and a deep student of human nature. He delighted in bringing out latent musical talent, wherever he could find it. He often taught pupils free, in cases where they were not able to pay.

"Van," as everybody who knew him affectionately called him, was always an inspiration in any company in which he was present, with his ready wit, his winning magnetism, and his cheery ways. It has been told me by those who could see, that when he was at the organ or piano, his face bore the happiest expression of any they had ever witnessed in like circumstances. He had his faults—and so have I mine—and as I suppose have all of us frail mortals: but notwithstanding these, we loved each other to the last.

S. Trevena Jackson, minister, writer, and close friend to Fanny Crosby, quoted the blind lady in 1915 as saying: "Now I am going to tell you something that only my closest friends know. I became a mother and knew a mother's love. God gave us a tender babe but the angels came down and took our infant up to God and to His throne."

In 1903, Fanny wrote about the duration of her marriage, "We were long spared bereavement: but he was taken sick in 1901, with asthma, and after a long illness, dies on June 18, 1902, of a complication of diseases.

"He was buried in Brooklyn, not far from where we first established our little home, soon after marriage; and there, though I cannot see the mound under which he rests, I can touch the turf with my hands, and try to make his spirit feel that I am constantly lamenting his temporary loss."

During their golden years, Fanny and her husband loved to think of their younger days together and share the thoughts that returned to their minds of little incidents that brought them mutual joy. One day when thumbing through the pages of a book, Fanny's fingers came upon a leaf pressed between the pages. She had no way of knowing for sure who put it there, but she knew in all likelihood that is was her husband. When and on what occasion he had picked the leaf, well, she didn't know that either, but she surmised it was at some special time when they had shared a love that can come only from God. Perhaps it was during a stroll beneath the trees that only God can build. For all Fanny knew, the leaf might have been plucked on that first walk they took on the campus of the New York Institution for the Blind. In any case, Fanny wrote of the leaf:

Only a Leaf

'Tis only a leaf, a withered leaf,
But its story is fraught with pain;
'Twas the gift of one who is far away,
And will never return again;
'Tis only a leaf, a withered leaf,
And yet I prize it so,
For it brings to my memory the brightest hour
I ever on earth shall know.

Ah, smile if you will; your lot is cast
Where pleasures around you twine,
And your heart in its gladness can never know
The grief that is breaking mine;
You have wealth and friends and a happy home,
With never a thought of gloom;
But my life is cold, and its hopes are dead,
And my heart is a living tomb.

He was all I had in the world to love,
He was all who cared for me;
And I watched his boat till I saw it sail
Like a speck on the broad blue sea;
And there came a voice, 'twas a dirgelike voice,
Out of the deep, dark wave;
And it told of one in a stranger land
That would sleep in a stranger's grave.

And I closed my eyes, and hid my face,
And uttered a low, sad cry,

As I laid me down on that lonely shore
And prayed that I might die;
And though my prayer was a selfish prayer,
I know it was all forgiven,
For a beam shot down that illumed my soul
From a pitying eye in heaven.

'Twas only a leaf, a withered leaf,
But I gaze on it o'er and o'er,
And I think of a hand that held it first,
A hand I shall clasp no more;
I know not how, but a message came,
A message that briefly said,
"Farewell, my own, it is over now;
The dream of our youth has fled."

I pressed the scroll to my burning lips,
And the leaf to my lonely breast
That beat and throbbed with an aching throb,
And was filled with a wild unrest;
And I still live on, like a captive bird
That pines in its cage so fair,
And longs for a breath from the orange groves,
And thinks that its mate is there.

'Tis only a leaf, a withered leaf,
But its story is fraught with pain;
'Twas the gift of one who is far away,
And will never return again;
He will never return; but I feel ere long
My spirit with his shall be,
And the old-time love shall be sweeter there
Where I know that he waits for me.

16
Fanny's First Hymn

Soon after resigning her teaching position at the New York Institution for the Blind, Fanny Crosby Van Alstyne compiled some of her writing and published her third book, *A Wreath of Columbia's Flowers*. This volume differs from her previous two in at least one important aspect—it contains some of her prose fiction stories, as well as poetry. Among these are "The Mountain Chief," "Annie Herbert," "Philip Synclare," and "Magerie."

From the day of her wedding in 1858 until late 1863, Fanny devoted full time to her duties as a wife and mother and did little writing. In December 1863, the Reverend Peter Stryker, minister of the Dutch Reformed Church, on Twenty-third Street, asked her to write a poem for the watch night service. Fanny gladly obliged, and the poem she wrote says:

The Old Year

Shall I weep for thee, Old Year?
I rejoiced when thou wert born;
And, with mirth and festive cheer,
How I hailed the blushing morn,
Cold and crisp, and yet so clear!
Shall I weep for thee, Old Year?

Thou art dying, and the bell
Soon will toll thy parting knell
Through the lonely, silent dell,
Where, with footstep light and free,
When the dew was on the lea,

And the violets came in spring,
Like a bird I used to sing;
But the winter now is here;
Shall I weep for thee, Old Year?

O the winter of the heart
When it hears the storm winds blow,
When it lays them 'neath the snow,
'Neath the white and feathery snow!
How it longs like thee to go!
For its days are dark and drear;
Shall I weep for thee, Old Year?

Thou art gone, and in thy place,
With a bright and smiling face,
Comes the New Year, fair as thou,
With a chaplet on his brow;
And his voice is sweet and clear;
Shall I weep for thee, Old Year?

But the spring will come ere long,
And my heart will then be gay,
When I hear the wild bird's song
As in many a bygone day,
And the sky will be as clear
As thine own, O vanished year.

A few days after the beginning of the new year, Mr. Stryker again came to Fanny and said, "Why don't you see Mr. Bradbury? He has told me more than once that he was looking for someone who could write hymns. I think you are the person for whom he has been looking, and I will give you a letter of introduction."

The Mr. Bradbury to whom Mr. Stryker referred was William B. Bradbury who, since 1860, was famous for hymns he had written, some including both words and music.

Mr. Bradbury was born on October 6, 1816, in York, Maine. Although he did not see an organ or piano until the age of seventeen, he inherited a great talent and desire for music from his parents, who were both excellent singers. He studied music under Lowell Mason. Later, he became a singing teacher and compiler of hymnals, the first one being *The Young Choir*, published in 1841. Some of his singing classes at festivals consisted of up to one thousand singing students! He also was known for writing a number of successful cantatas. Mr. Bradbury studied abroad in 1847 and 1849. In 1854 he and his brother, Edward, and a German piano maker established a piano business, under the firm name of Lighte, Newton and Bradbury Piano Company. The business was later absorbed by the Knabe Piano Company, and William Bradbury continued teaching and writing sacred music.

When Mr. Stryker offered to introduce Fanny to Mr. Bradbury, she was overjoyed and gladly agreed to visit Mr. Bradbury in his office at 425 Broome Street.

On February 2, 1864, the blind lady made her way to that address.

"Fanny," Mr. Bradbury said, "I thank God that we have at last met; for I think you can write hymns; and I have wished for a long time to have a talk with you."

At the end of the interview, Fanny promised to bring him words for a hymn within the week, and three days later she returned with the following verses:

Our Bright Home Above

We are going, we are going
To a home beyond the skies,
Where the fields are robed in beauty,
And the sunlight never dies;
Where the fount of joy is flowing
In the valley green and fair,
We shall dwell in love together;
There will be no parting there.

We are going, we are going,
And the music we have heard
Like the echo of the woodland,
Or the carol of a bird;

With the rosy light of morning,
On the calm and fragrant air,
Still it murmurs, softly murmurs,
There will be no parting there.

We are going, we are going,
When the day of life is o'er,
To that pure and happy region
Where our friends have gone before;
They are singing with the angels
In that land so bright and fair;
We shall dwell with them forever;
There will be no parting there.

Mr. Bradbury set the words to music and Fanny's first hymn was ready for publication! It appeared on page seventy-one of William Bradbury's *Golden Censer,* a hymnal published that same year, 1864.

17
Lifetime Employment

Fanny's first hymn, published in William B. Bradbury's hymnal *Golden Censer*, met with immediate success. She was pleased to be associated with such a great name in the gospel music field, and she praised God for continuing his work in her life.

Mr. Bradbury, however, didn't wait until the first hymn was published to ask for another. Within a week of the time that Fanny delivered the verses for "Our Bright Home Above," Mr. Bradbury sent for her again.

In 1864 the great Civil War had been in progress for three long years, and it was never certain what the outcome of that conflict would be. Second probably only to her Christian experience was Fanny Crosby's patriotism. So when Mr. Bradbury's second request was for a patriotic song, it pleased Fanny almost as much as his first request. He suggested the title "A Sound Among the Mulberry Trees," but Fanny timidly suggested that "There's a Sound Among the Forest Trees" would be better and Mr. Bradbury gladly consented to her idea.

The music had already been written, and Fanny at first thought it somewhat difficult; but after hearing it played two or three times, she was able to count the measure and adapt the words to the music.

When the words were in their completed state, Fanny carried them to the office. Mr. Bradbury was out at the moment but his bookkeeper played the song through and exclaimed, "How in the world did you manage to write that hymn? Nobody ever supposed that you, or any other mortal, could adapt words to that melody."

Mr. Bradbury entered the room about that time and looked over the hymn.

"Fanny," he said, "I am surprised beyond measure; and, now, let me say that as long as I have a publishing house, you will always have work."

At the age of forty-four, Fanny Crosby was a writer of hymns. She went home and that evening sat in her room, reflecting on those forty-four years. The pieces of the puzzle were falling into place: The complete surrender of her life to God's will a few years ago; her teaching career; her study of the great poets and their work; her education at the Institution; her memory development; the fifteen years prior to her formal schooling, in which she learned so many of the Scriptures. Fanny even thought of her life at the age of six weeks, when the Lord "permitted" her to be blind. She later said that she believed she would never have written a hymn had she had normal physical sight. And Fanny thanked God for the privilege that was hers!

One day the words "I will sing of the mercies of the Lord for ever" (Ps. 89:1) came to Fanny Crosby's mind. She sat down and penned the following words and Mr. Bradbury set them to music, under the title of "Mercy":

> I'll sing the glory of the Lord,
> His Goodness I'll proclaim;
> And tell how great His mercies are
> To those that fear His name:
>
> Up to the everlasting hills,
> I'll lift my waiting eyes,
> And there with early morning light,
> My grateful prayer shall rise.
>
> I'll sing of Christ, the Holy One,
> Who bore the cross for me;
> His all-atoning sacrifice
> My precious theme shall be.

High on His throne exalted now
He sits at God's right hand;
The only refuge of my soul,
The Rock on which I stand.

I'll sing the mercy of the Lord,
And praise Him while I've breath;
I'll trust in Him whose rod and staff
Will comfort me in death.
Dissolve, O earthly house of clay,
And let my spirit soar.
With all the ransomed hosts above
To praise Him evermore.

This fine hymn was published and was popular for many years.

Fanny Crosby loved children and Mr. Bradbury worked with thousands of them in his singing classes. It was only natural, then, that many of their hymns were written for children. Fanny wrote a patriotic one and this one, too, appears in *Golden Censer:*

Our Fathers Long Ago

When across the ocean wide,
Where the heaving waters flow,
Came the Mayflower o'er the tide,
With our fathers, long ago;
When they neared the rocky strand,
And their chorus rent the air,
Children in that pilgrim band
Clasped their little hands in prayer.

Sweetly rang their evening hymn
O'er that region vast and wide,
Through the forest dark and dim,
And the rocking pines replied,
'Twas a cold December night,
And the earth was robed in snow,
But the stars with mellow light
Blest our fathers long ago.

When the early buds were seen,
And the robin's song was heard,
Children frolicked on the green,
Happy as the woodland bird;
Culled the daisy young and fair,
Watched the brooklet's quiet flow,
Banished every cloud of care
From our fathers long ago.

When our country's banner bright
Told her deeds of noble worth,
Children hailed its radiant light,
Hailed the land that gave them birth,
Children now rejoice to hear,
All their youthful hearts can know,
And the precepts still revere
Of their fathers long ago.

Fanny J. Crosby in 1912

EVANGELISTS.

Mrs. P. P. Bliss.   Ira D. Sankey.   Mr. P. P. Bliss.
D. W. Whittle.   D. L. Moody.   G. C. Stebbins.
Henry Morehouse.

An array of Fanny's hymn-writing and evangelistic friends—
D. L. Moody, Ira D. Sankey, Mr. and Mrs. P. P. Bliss, G. C.
Stebbins, D. W. Whittle, and Henry Morehouse

Other people who figured in Miss Crosby's life—(Top, left) Jenny Lind (Top, right) George Frederick Root (Bottom, left) Mrs. Joseph F. Knapp, and (Bottom, right) President Grover Cleveland

(Top) The Hudson River, much as it looked when Fanny made her first trip to New York (Bottom) Fanny's birthplace as it is today

Carnegie Hall where Fanny J. Crosby, at 91, appeared before an audience of 5,000

18
The Sunlight Never Dies

The patriotic-type hymn "There's a Sound Among the Forest Trees" was used for the duration of the Civil War and brought comfort and enthusiasm to soldiers and their families alike. But when that terrible conflict was over, Fanny Crosby one day asked Mr. Bradbury, "What are you going to do with 'Forest Trees'?"

"What can we do with it?" he asked in return.

"Oh," she replied, "we can write sacred words to the melody; and indeed the subject comes to me now: 'There's a Cry from Macedonia.' " Mr. Bradbury gladly gave his permission and Fanny wrote a missionary hymn that was very popular. The first verse and chorus are:

> The light of the Gospel bring, O come!
> Let us hear the joyful tidings of salvation,
> We thirst for the living spring.
> O ye heralds of the cross be up and doing,
> Remember the great command, away!
> Go ye forth and preach the word to every creature,
> Proclaim it in ever land.
>
> They shall gather from the East
> They shall gather from the West,
> With the patriachs of old,
> And the ransomed shall return
> To the kingdoms of the blest
> With their harps and crowns of gold.
>
> There's a cry from Macedonia—Come and help us;

The light of the Gospel bring, O come!
Let us hear the joyful tidings of salvation,
We thirst for the living spring.

Mr. Bradbury sometimes would give Fanny a title and ask her to write a hymn on the subject and adapt them to a melody he had already written. But more often she was allowed to select her own subject. Fanny Crosby had a marvelous talent in meter and rhyme and part of her duties in her employment with Mr. Bradbury consisted of revising lyrics that others had written and adapting them to Mr. Bradbury's music.

Fanny wrote "Strike the Harp of Zion" for a lively tune composed by Mr. Bradbury and it was published in *Bright Jewels*, in 1869:

Strike the harp of Zion, wake the tuneful lay;
Bear the joyful tidings far away;
Lo! the morn is breaking, morn of purest love,
Praise forever, praise to God above.

Glory! glory! hark! the angels sing,
Glory! glory! hear the echo ring!
Strike the harp of Zion, wake the tuneful lay;
Bear the joyful tidings far away.

Over distant regions vailed in error's night,
See the holy dawn of gospel light;
See! the nations coming at the Saviour's call,
Coming now to crown Him Lord of all.

O, the joyful story, life to every soul!
Like a mighty ocean let it roll,
Bringing home the lost ones from the path of sin,
Till the world shall all be gathered in.

This musical team worked together and produced many hymns and gospel songs that were well received. In April 1866 however, Mr. Bradbury became seriously ill and went South for three months to recuperate.

He returned with increased strength, but the doctors and his friends were forced to admit that his life was gradually being taken by a disease the doctors diagnosed as consumption, later generally known as tuberculosis.

One afternoon in the fall of 1867, Mr. Bradbury called Fanny to him and said, "These interviews have been very pleasant to me, but they will soon be over; I am going to be forever with the Lord; and I will await you on the bank of the river."

Greatly distressed by his words, Fanny replied, "Oh must I lose a friendship that I have enjoyed so much?"

"No," he answered, "take up my lifework where I lay it down; and you will not indeed lose a friendship, though I am going away from you, but rather strengthen it by striving to carry out my own ideals."

As the weeks went by, Mr. Bradbury became weaker, and at sunset on January 7, 1868, he passed away. He was loved by children everywhere, for he had taught thousands of them in his singing classes. Some of them made a wreath of oak leaves and laid it on his casket, and as blind Fanny Crosby stood there, tears streaming down her cheeks, she heard a voice from somewhere in the congregation say, "Fanny, pick up the work where Mr. Bradbury leaves it; take your harp from the willow, and dry your tears."

Fanny never learned who spoke those words, but somehow they strengthened her. And she was determined to follow the advice. A peaceful rest came over her when the congregation started singing the first hymn that she and William B. Bradbury wrote:

> We are going, we are going,
> To a home beyond the skies,
> Where the fields are robed in beauty,
> And the sunlight never dies.

19
More Hymns

When William B. Bradbury advised Fanny Crosby to "take up my lifework where I lay it down," he didn't leave her without someone to work with. She met L. H. Biglow and renewed her acquaintance with Sylvester Main (mentioned in an earlier chapter as being a friend of hers in childhood) about the same time she wrote her first hymn for William Bradbury. Others she met while working with Mr. Bradbury include Theodore E. Perkins, Hubert P. Main (son of Sylvester), Mrs. Joseph F. Knapp, T. F. Seward, C. G. Allen, W. H. Doane, and Philip Phillips. With Mr. Bradbury's permission, she had already written words for music by some of these composers. The day after Mr. Bradbury's funeral, she met W. F. Sherwin.

Most of the people Fanny worked with were famous in their day and many of their names are familiar today. Certainly Philip Phillips is no exception. He was born in Chautauqua County, New York, in 1834, and studied under Lowell Mason. During the Civil War he sang for the Christian Commission. In 1866 he became editor of the Methodist Book Concern. He was later a singing evangelist and toured the world singing in 1872. He was author of many hymns and compiled a number of great hymnals, including *Early Blossoms, Musical Leaves, Hallowed Songs, Our Musical Favorite,* and *The Singing Pilgrim.*

At the Hall of Representatives in Washington, D. C., Mr. Phillips sang a gospel hymn entitled "Your Mission." The words were written by Mrs. Ellen H. Gates, and the first verse states:

If you can not on the ocean
Sail among the swiftest fleet,
Rocking on the highest billows,
Laughing at the storms you meet,
You can stand among the sailors,
Anchored yet within the bay;
You can lend a hand to help them,
As you launch their boat away.

The date of the singing was February 29, 1865, just a few short weeks before President Lincoln was assassinated. And the President was in the audience. When Mr. Phillips concluded his singing, President Lincoln scribbled a note and sent it to the Honorable William H. Seward:

"Near the close let us have 'Your Mission' repeated by Mr. Phillips. Don't say I called for it. A. Lincoln."

Mr. Phillips was later associated with Dwight L. Moody. Philip Phillips was familiarly known as "The Singing Pilgrim," and when he was compiling his book by that name in 1866, he sent Fanny Crosby a list of forty titles and asked her to write words on those subjects. It was then that Fanny performed an amazing feat involving the remarkable memory she developed early in life when she memorized entire books of the Bible and scores of fine poems. She composed the entire list of forty hymns and retained them all in her memory, not writing any on paper until all forty were in their finished state. After Mr. Phillips published them that year in *The Singing Pilgrim*, he asked for and received an additional forty for a subsequent book. These were composed in the same manner.

One among the many hymns written by Fanny Crosby and Philip Phillips was "Oh, What Are You Going to Do?" Not only was it widely used in the United States, but Ira D. Sankey, the singer with the Moody evangelistic team, introduced it in England and it became popular there. It was published in 1867 and the first verse states:

Oh, what are you going to do, brother?
Say, what are you going to do?

> You have thought of some useful labor,
> But what is the end in view.
> You are fresh from the home of your boyhood,
> And just in the bloom of youth!
> Have you tasted the sparkling water
> That flows from the fount of truth?

After Mr. Bradbury died in 1868, the name of the company was changed to Biglow and Main, with L. H. Biglow as senior member and Sylvester Main was his partner. Rev. Robert Lowry became editor, with William F. Sherwin and Chester G. Allen his assistants. W. Howard Doane composed much of the music and his name, too, soon appeared on the title pages of some of the hymnals the company published.

Among the first hymnals published by the newly organized company was *Bright Jewels*. In it, the first paragraph of the introduction states:

From the old and well-known House which has already supplied the Sunday Schools of our land with 4,000,000 of Music Books, we greet you with a new Song Book of *Bright Jewels*, to aid you in your blessed employment. We have aimed to make it worthy of acceptance among those to whom spirituality of thought and purity of expression are among the chief elements of value in Sunday School song.

One among Fanny Crosby's many hymns included in the book is "A Jewel Worth Keeping." It was set to music by William F. Sherwin:

> I know of a jewel whose lustre
> Is purer and brighter than gold—
> A Jewel that sparkles forever,
> Adorning the young and the old;
> A Jewel more precious than rubies,
> Or pearls from the depth of the sea—
> A Jewel, dear children, worth keeping,
> A treasure for you and for me.

A Jewel, dear Children, worth keeping,
A treasure for you and for me;
A Jewel, dear Children, worth keeping,
A treasure for you and for me.

That Jewel, the *love* that redeems us!
O seek it by watching and prayer;
I know the dear Saviour is willing
To give you that Jewel so fair:
And O, in the crown of the faithful,
Its glory transcendent shall be—
A Jewel, dear children, worth keeping,
A treasure for you and for me.

20
Still More Hymns

Probably every Christian that has ever lived has had valley and mountaintop experiences in his daily Christian life, and Fanny Crosby was no exception. She, however, believed that even the valley experiences were for a purpose and it seems her belief has proved correct.

At a great revival meeting one night in 1868 it seemed to Fanny that all those near her and throughout the great auditorium were receiving bountiful blessings from the Holy Spirit, while her own heart ached with loneliness. Then it seemed to her that her very soul cried out, "Savior, do not pass me by!" A great peace and joy came upon her, and that night she wrote the words to one of her most successful hymns, "Pass Me Not":

Pass me not, O gentle Saviour,
Hear my humble cry;
While on others Thou art smiling,
Do not pass me by.

Saviour, Saviour,
Hear my humble cry,
While on others Thou art calling,
Do not pass me by.

William H. Doane set the words to music, as he did with many of her popular hymns. Ira D. Sankey, the singer that toured much of the world with Dwight L. Moody, said of the hymn:

No hymn in our collection was more popular than this at our meetings in London in 1874. It was sung almost every day in Her Majesty's Theater, in Pall Mall, and has been translated into several languages.

At one of our noonday prayer meetings in Glasgow a prominent gentleman was awakened by the singing of this hymn. He had been very much opposed to our meetings, and his opposition was not lessened when he saw his wife converted. That day he had agreed to attend the meeting for the last time, as a sort of concession; and that was the day when the Spirit of God touched him by this hymn.

Fanny's story about meeting Mr. Doane is an interesting one:

In the year 1867 I met Dr. William H. Doane under very interesting circumstances. He had come from his home in Cincinnati to New York to visit his friend Dr. Van Meter of the Five Points Mission; and they were looking for a hymn that might be used on a certain anniversary. A number of standard hymns were given Mr. Doane, but he did not find them appropriate. About this time I had been writing "More Like Jesus"; and Dr. Lowry asked me why I did not send it to Mr. Doane. I said, "Well, I will," and accordingly sent it by a messenger boy. The latter handed my words to Mr. Doane, who happened to be at the moment talking with Dr. Van Meter; and he laid them down for a few minutes. When he took up the letter and glanced over its contents he started after the boy, but could not find him. He returned to Dr. Van Meter disheartened, but determined to find me if I was anywhere to be found in the city. He again went out and hunted for me the rest of the day; and it was not until about eight or nine in the evening that he was finally directed to my boarding place. I went to the door, and he asked, "Are you Fanny Crosby?" On being informed I was that person, he said, "Oh, how glad I am to find you; I have been trying to do so a long while, and at last I have succeeded."

Mr. Doane placed in Fanny's hand what she supposed to be a two-dollar bill. Later, however, she found that it was twenty dollars and tried to return the bill to him.

"The Lord sent that hymn," he said, "and meant that you should have the twenty dollars for it."

The hymn was published on page ninety-seven of *Pure Gold:*

> More like Jesus would I be;
> Let my Saviour dwell with me,
> Fill my soul with peace and love,
> Make me gentle as the dove;
> More like Jesus while I go,
> Pilgrim in this world below;
> Poor in spirit would I be—
> Let my Saviour dwell in me.
>
> If He hears the raven's cry,
> If His ever-watchful eye
> Marks the sparrows when they fall,
> Surely He will hear my call;
> He will teach me how to live,
> All my sinful thoughts forgive;
> Pure in heart I still would be—
> Let my Saviour dwell in me.
>
> More like Jesus when I pray,
> More like Jesus day by day,
> May I rest me by His side,
> Where the tranquil waters glide;
> Born of Him, through grace renewed,
> By his love my will subdued,
> Rich in faith I still would be—
> Let my Saviour dwell in me.

One cold rainy day Fanny Crosby was sitting in her room, while a friend stood at the window, looking out. "Is there any sign of clearing?" Fanny asked. The clouds had parted just enough to let a beam of light come shining through. "There's only a beam of sunshine," the friend replied, "but, oh, it's warm and bright!"

These words wouldn't leave Fanny, and as she rocked in her chair she composed the following lines, and they were set to music by John R. Sweney:

> Only a beam of sunshine,
> But oh, it was warm and bright;
> The heart of a weary traveler,
> Was cheered by its welcome sight.
> Only a beam of sunshine
> That fell from the arch above,
> And tenderly, softly whispered
> A message of peace and love.
>
> Only a beam of sunshine
> That into a dwelling crept,
> Where over a fading rosebud,
> A mother her vigil kept.
>
> Only a beam of sunshine
> That smiled through her falling tears,
> And showed her the bow of promise,
> Forgotten perhaps for years.
>
> Only a word for Jesus!
> Oh, speak it in His dear name;
> To perishing souls around you
> The message of love proclaim.
> Go, like the faithful sunbeam,
> Your mission of joy fulfill;
> Remember the Saviour's promise,
> That He will be with you still.

Fanny Crosby was visiting in the home of Mr. William H. Doane one evening, and as the sun was setting behind the hills the two were talking of the nearness of God. The sunset described by Mr. Doane and the subject they discussed so impressed Fanny Crosby that she wrote "I Am Thine, O Lord." Mr. Doane wrote the music. The hymn says:

> I am thine, O Lord, I have heard Thy voice,
> And it told Thy love to me;
> But I long to rise in the arms of faith,
> And be closer drawn to Thee.
>
> Draw me nearer, nearer, blessed Lord,
> To the cross where Thou hast died;
> Draw me nearer, nearer, nearer, blessed Lord,
> To Thy precious bleeding side.
>
> Consecrate me now to Thy service, Lord,
> By the power of grace divine;
> Let my soul look up with a steadfast hope,
> And my will be lost in Thine.
>
> O the pure delight of a single hour
> That before Thy throne I spend,
> When I kneel in prayer, and with Thee, my God,
> I commune as friend with friend!
>
> There are depths of love that I cannot know
> Till I cross the narrow sea,
> There are heights of joy that I may not reach
> Till I rest in peace with Thee.

21
And Still More Hymns

"I may be able, sometime, to remember the names of all those who have done my hymns the honor of setting them to music," Fanny Crosby wrote in 1903, "but have not the leisure just at present."

Looking through hymnals published from 1864 up to the present date, one can see why it would be difficult to name them all. While most of her hymns, including the ones that have endured the years, probably were set to music by eight or ten people, there are hundreds of other hymns for which the music was written by musicians almost too numerous to name. The difficulty of this task is increased because Fanny wrote under many noms de plume and some of the musicians may not have set more than one or two of her hymns to music. Also, her production was so vast that some of her writing probably never appeared in more than one or two books and has long since been out of print.

It was mentioned in a previous chapter that Fanny's husband, Alexander Van Alstyne, wrote the music for some of her compositions. Few, if any, of these are carried in current hymnals. Whether the lyrics or music failed to meet the standards of the years or whether the two were not suitable one for the other, I cannot say. It may have been simply that through the years such a staggering number of hymns has been written that some, including these, of necessity had to be dropped.

One for which Fanny's husband wrote the music appeared in *Pure Gold*. The title is "Stay Thee, Weary Child," and the final verse states:

O the joy, the bliss of heaven
O'er a soul returning!
Shall the legions there,
Strike their harps for thee?
Come, O weary child of sin,
Jesus waits to let thee in;
Hear Him say, "Come Away,"
Grace, grace is free.

William J. Kirkpatrick was a master at composing hymnal music, and did so for some of Fanny's hymns. One that the reader no doubt will instantly recognize is:

A wonderful Saviour is Jesus my Lord,
A wonderful Saviour to me,
He hideth my soul in the cleft of the rock,
Where rivers of pleasure I see.

He hideth my soul in the cleft of the rock
That shadows a dry, thirsty land;
He hideth my life in the depths of His love,
And covers me there with His hand.

A wonderful Saviour is Jesus my Lord,
He taketh my burden away,
He holdeth me up, and I shall not be moved,
He giveth me strength as my day.

With numberless blessings each moment He crowns,
And filled with His goodness divine,
I sing in my rapture, oh, glory to God
For such a redeemer as mine!

When clothed in His brightness, transported I rise
To meet Him in clouds of the sky,
His perfect salvation, His wonderful love,
I'll shout with the millions on high.

Fanny was often asked how it was possible that she wrote so many hymns. Here are some comments on the subject, in Fanny Crosby's own words:

That some of my hymns have been dictated by the blessed Holy Spirit I have no doubt; and that others have been the result of deep meditation I know to be true; but that the poet has any right to claim special merit for himself is certainly presumptuous. I have sometimes felt that there was a deep and clear well of inspiration from which one may draw the sparkling draughts that are so essential to good poetry. At times the burden of inspiration is so heavy that the author himself cannot find words beautiful enough, or thoughts deep enough, for its expression.

Most of my poems have been written during the long night watches, when the distractions of the day could not interfere with the rapid flow of thought. It has been my custom to hold a little book in my hand; and somehow or other the words seem to come more promptly when I am so engaged. I can also remember more accurately when the little volume is in my grasp. Many people, noting this peculiar custom, have asked some queer questions about it; and not a few fancy that I may indeed be able to see what is printed there. Sometimes a hymn comes to me by stanzas and needs only to be written down, but I never have any portion of a poem committed to paper until the entire poem is composed; then there is often much pruning and revising necessary before it is really finished. Some poems, it is true, come as a complete whole, and need no revision— indeed the best seem to come that way—but the great majority do not.

It may seem a little old fashioned, always to begin one's work with prayer; but I never undertake a hymn without first asking the good Lord to be my inspiration in the work that I am about to do.

Many of Fanny's hymns were her "soul's sincere desire," and were, therefore, prayers. One, for example, was her "Come, Great Deliverer, Come," set to music by W. H. Doane. The first and last verses say:

O hear my cry, be gracious now to me,
Come, Great Deliverer come;
My soul bowed down is longing now for Thee,
Come, Great Deliverer come.

Thou wilt not spurn contrition's broken sigh,
Come Great Deliverer, come;
Regard my prayer, and hear my humble cry,
Come Great Deliverer, come.

Refrain: I've wandered far away o'er mountains cold,
I've wandered far away from home;
O take me now, and bring me to Thy fold,
Come, Great Deliverer come.

Fanny Crosby believed in the power of prayer, and the results of some of her prayers inspired some of her hymns. On one such occasion Fanny was alone at home and there arose a desperate need for the sum of five dollars. Those to whom she normally would go for such help were out of the city, attending a convention. It came to her mind that she should pray for the money, so she knelt at her bedside and did so. She did not ask for three dollars, because that amount was not enough. She did not ask for ten dollars because she had no need for that much. She prayed specifically for five dollars. She then arose and went about her household chores, fully confident that her need would be met or that it was not God's will for her to have the money—and she was willing to accept that.

At this stage in Fanny's life she had become quite famous for her hymns. Sometimes a stranger would look her up just to meet the lady who had written so many fine hymns. Shortly after her prayer that day there came a knock at her door. A gentleman there spoke briefly with her, shook her hand, and departed. As she closed the door, she realized he had left something in her hand. It proved to be exactly five dollars —not a cent less, not a cent more! Fanny sat in her favorite chair and these words poured from her heart, line for line:

All the way my Saviour leads me;
What have I to ask beside?
Can I doubt His tender mercy,
Who through life has been my guide?
Heavenly peace, divinest comfort,
Here by faith in Him to dwell!
For I know whate'er befall me,
Jesus doeth all things well.

All the way my Saviour leads me,
Cheers each winding path I tread;
Gives me grace for ever trial,
Feeds me with the living bread;
Though my weary steps may falter,
And my soul athirst may be,
Gushing from the Rock before me,
Lo, a spring of joy I see.

All the way my Saviour leads me;
O the fullness of His love!
Perfect rest to me is promised
In my Father's house above;
When my spirit, clothed, immortal,
Wings its flight to realms of day,
This my song through endless ages—
Jesus led me all the way.

22
Blessed Assurance

It was mentioned in another chapter that Fanny Crosby memorized eight complete books of the Bible and on at least two occasions she composed hymns in groups of forty and retained them all in her memory before writing any of them on paper. In spite of her remarkable memory, however, it was impossible to always remember all the hymns she had written, and this sometimes proved embarrassing for her.

In 1906 Fanny wrote:

Among the great number of hymns that I have written—eight thousand perhaps—it is not always possible for me to remember even the best of them. For this reason I have made laughable mistakes. One morning, for example, at Northfield the audience sang "Hide Me, O My Saviour, Hide Me." But I did not recognize this hymn as my own production; and therefore I may be pardoned for saying that I was much pleased with it. Turning to Mr. Sankey (who had played it) I asked, "Where did you get that piece?" He paid no particular attention to my question, for he supposed I was merely joking; and at that moment the bell called us to dinner,—so both of us forgot about the hymn. But it was again used at the afternoon service; and then I was determined to know who wrote it.

"Mr. Sankey," I said, "Now you must tell me who is the author of that piece."

"Really," he replied, "don't you recall who wrote that hymn? You ought to remember, for you are the guilty one."

W. H. Doane wrote the music. The words are:

> Hide me, O my Saviour hide me
> In Thy holy place;
> Resting there beneath Thy glory,
> O let me see Thy face.
>
> O blessed Saviour, hide me;
> O Saviour, keep me Safely, O Lord, with Thee,
> O my Saviour, keep Thou me.
>
> Hide me, when the storm is raging
> O'er life's troubled sea;
> Like a dove on ocean's billows,
> O let me fly to Thee.
>
> Hide me, when my heart is breaking
> With its weight of woe;
> When in tears I seek the comfort
> Thou canst alone bestow.

Fanny wrote "Dark Is the Night" and it was published in *Gospel Hymns No. 2* in 1876. This hymn, popular for many years, was set to music by T. E. Perkins. Ira D. Sankey of the Moody Evangelistic Team wrote of this hymn in *My Life and Story of the Gospel Hymns:* "When I was chorister in Mr. Moody's Sunday School, on the north side of Chicago, we frequently used this hymn."

Mr. Sankey wrote further about how he also used this hymn during the great Chicago fire. While it was raging, he climbed into a small boat and rowed out on Lake Michigan to escape the intense heat and possible death. Sitting there, rocked by the waves, Mr. Sankey watched the city burn. And while he watched, he sang:

> Dark is the night, and cold the wind is blowing,
> Nearer and nearer comes the breakers' roar;
> Where shall I go, or whither fly for refuge?
> Hide me, my Father, till the storm is o'er.

> Dark is the night, but cheering is the promise;
> He will go with me o'er the troubled wave;
> Safe He will lead me through the pathless waters,
> Jesus, the mighty one, and strong to save.
>
> Dark is the night, but lo! the day is breaking,
> Onward my bark, unfurl the every sail;
> Now at the helm I see my Father standing,
> Soon will my anchor drop within the vail.

Near the turn of the century in the South there was a prominent man visiting in a small town not far from his home. Passing a church one evening he heard the congregation singing and decided to go in and hear a hymn or two. He heard only one and left. The words, however, did not leave him. They kept repeating themselves, over and over. The following day he could still hear the singing, just as clearly, it seemed, as when the congregation sang the hymn. Finally it led to his conviction, repentance, and rebirth in Christ.

The hymn was written by Fanny Crosby and set to music by W. H. Doane. The words as they appeared in *Gospel Hymns No. 2* in 1871 are:

> Only a step to Jesus!
> Then why not take it now?
> Come, and, thy sin confessing,
> To Him thy Saviour bow.
>
> Only a step, Only a step;
> Come, He waits for Thee;
> Come, and, thy sin confessing
> Thou shalt receive a blessing
> Do not reject the mercy
> He freely offers thee.
>
> Only a step to Jesus!
> Believe, and thou shalt live;
> Lovingly now He's waiting,
> And ready to forgive.

Only a step to Jesus!
A step from sin to grace;
What hast thy heart decided?
The moments fly apace.

Only a step to Jesus!
O why not come, and say,
Gladly to Thee, my Saviour,
I give myself away.

In 1906 Ira D. Sankey related a story in connection with two hymns, one of which was written by Fanny Crosby. The story involved British soldiers in the province of Transvaal in South Africa. It was during the South African War, and when a group of soldiers on their way to the front met another group, they had a sort of secret code they used to relay a certain greeting or message. One group would call to the others, "Four-nine-four, boys; four-nine-four!" Someone in the other group would reply, "Six further on, boys; six further on!" The numbers, Mr. Sankey said, corresponded to the numbers of two hymns in a pocket hymnal, *Sacred Songs & Solos*, which the soldiers carried. Four-nine-four was number 494, of course, and six further on was number 500.

In doing research for this biography, I located a copy of that small but thick volume compiled by Ira D. Sankey and obtained it for my personal library. The book contains 750 hymns and number 494 is "God Be With You Till We Meet Again," and number 500 is Fanny Crosby's hymn "Blessed Assurance, Jesus Is Mine!"

"Blessed Assurance, Jesus Is Mine" has been, and no doubt still is, one of the most loved hymns that Fanny wrote. Whether the words make up a poem that some great poet would judge good, I do not know. And what has made it survive the years, I do not know. But I do feel that it is a testimony that came from the heart of a blind Christian lady more than a hundred years ago, and it is, no doubt, a typical testimony of every born-again Christian.

As was the case with many of Fanny's finest hymns, the words of this one came after the music was written. The music was composed by Mrs. Joseph F. Knapp, whose husband founded the Metropolitan Life Insurance Company of New York.

Mrs. Knapp, a devout Christian and skilled musician came to Fanny's house one day in 1873, with the music she had written. She sat at the piano and played the melody through once and as she started the second time she asked Fanny, "What does the music say to you? Do you hear any words?"

Leaning back in her rocking chair, with her blind eyes closed, Fanny replied, "I hear, 'Blessed Assurance, Jesus Is Mine!'" And as Mrs. Knapp continued to play, Fanny rocked to the rhythm, and the words poured from her lips, almost line for line:

> Blessed assurance, Jesus is mine,
> O what a foretaste of glory divine!
> Heir of salvation, purchase of God,
> Born of His spirit, washed in His blood;
> This is my story, this is my song,
> Praising my Saviour all the day long.

23
Fanny's Finest Hour

Probably no other person has been associated with such a long list of great people in the gospel hymn writing business as was Fanny Crosby. At the peak of her career she worked with Victor H. Benke, William J. Kirkpatrick, Mrs. Joseph F. Knapp, Hubert P. Main, James McGranahan, Philip Phillips, Josephine Pollard, Henry Tucker, Theodore F. Seward, William F. Sherwin, John R. Sweney, H. R. Palmer, Mrs. Agnes Woolston, Silas J. Vail, Mrs. Clark Wilson, Eliza E. Hewitt, James M. Black, William B. Bradbury, Philip P. Bliss, George F. Bristow, Henry Brown, Mrs. Lanta Wilson Smith, George Stebbins, B. C. Unseld, J. W. Vandeventer, W. S. Weeden, Clark Wilson, John R. Clements, Mary Upham Currier, H. P. Danks, William H. Doane, Charles H. Gabriel, Adam Geibel, Harriet E. Jones, Mary A. Kidder, Robert Lowry, Sylvester Main, David Wood, Theodore E. Perkins, W. A. Post, Ira D. Sankey, and I. Allan Sankey.

Some of these were lyric writers, but most of them were musicians who set to music thousands of hymns that Fanny Crosby wrote. The list is not complete, of course, but if one of Fanny's gospel songs is looked up in any hymnal one of the above names is likely to be opposite hers.

To what extent Fanny Crosby and Philip P. Bliss would have worked together had he lived more than thirty-eight years no one knows. He was a gifted poet and musician and wrote both words and music to many all-time greats, such as "Wonderful Words of Life," "Almost Persuaded," and "Let the Lower Lights Be Burning."

The story of how one of his hymns was written is a touching

one. Mrs. H. G. Spafford, wife of a Chicago businessman, and her four children were aboard the French Steamer *Ville de Havre* when it collided with another ship and sank within thirty minutes. As the ship settled lower and lower into the foaming billows, Mrs. Spafford gathered her children around her and knelt in prayer. The children were never seen again, but the mother was found floating among the flotsam. She was pulled aboard a boat and revived. At her first opportunity she wired her husband, "Saved alone."

Mr. Spafford, naturally, was grief stricken. He was, however, soon able to accept the tragedy as the Lord's will and not long afterward wrote a poem in memory of his children. Mr. Bliss set it to music and the first verse of the hymn, "It Is Well With My Soul," states:

> When peace, like a river, attendeth my way,
> When sorrows like sea billows roll;
> Whatever my lot, Thou hast taught me to say,
> It is well, it is well with my soul.

Soon after the hymn was published, Mr. Bliss attended a meeting and when it came time for his final song, he said, "I may not be coming this way again," and he sang a song entitled "I'm Going Home Tomorrow."

The following day he and his wife died in a spectacular train wreck and their bodies along with a hundred others were never accounted for.

On April 30, 1868, W. H. Doane came to Fanny's house. "I have exactly forty minutes before my train leaves for Cincinnati," he said. "Here is a melody," and he sat down at the piano. "Can you write words for it?"

He began playing and Fanny Crosby settled into her chair and breathed a prayer. And as the beautiful music came to her ears, words flowed from her lips:

> Safe in the arms of Jesus,
> Safe on His gentle breast,

> There by His love o'ershaded,
> Sweetly my soul shall rest.
> Hark! 'tis the voice of angels,
> Borne in a song to me,
> Over the fields of glory,
> Over the jasper sea.

Forty minutes from the time he arrived at Fanny's house, Dr. Doane was climbing aboard the train and on his way to the Sunday School convention in Cincinnati. In his pocket he had the words to one of Fanny Crosby's most beautiful hymns—just as they stand today! Fanny later claimed "Safe in the Arms of Jesus" as her own personal favorite of all she wrote.

Fanny told a story of how one of her great hymns almost failed to be published. One summer while Dwight L. Moody was in Europe, the Northfield Conventions were left in charge of Dr. A. J. Gordon and Ira D. Sankey. One day Mr. Sankey came to Fanny and asked her to give a brief speech. She felt she was not prepared to speak before such a vast audience, with no advance notice.

"Oh, Mr. Sankey, I cannot speak before such an array of talent," she said.

Dr. Pierson, also on the program, said, "Yes, you can. There is no one here of whom you need be afraid."

"Fanny," Dr. Gordon asked, "do you speak to please man or to please God?"

"Why, I hope to please God," Fanny answered.

"Well, then," Dr. Gordon said, "go out and do your duty."

Fanny spoke to the audience for a few minutes and closed her remarks with some verses of a hymn she remembered writing a few years before:

> Some day the silver cord will break,
> And I no more as now shall sing;
> But, O the joy when I shall wake
> Within the palace of the King!"

"Fanny, where did you get that poem," Mr. Sankey asked when she returned to her seat.

"Why, I wrote it for the Biglow and Main Company (the company that Fanny Crosby and Ira Sankey were associated with) two years ago," she said.

By this time Fanny was so prolific in her writing that many of her hymns were stored in a safe for later use. Mr. Sankey lost no time in digging this one out. It was set to music by George C. Stebbins and became one of Fanny Crosby's most loved hymns.

In another chapter it was stated that someone standing near the window when showers of rain had ended remarked "There is only a beam of sunshine, but, oh, it is warm and bright," and that simple statement inspired Fanny to write a hymn. Many of her other hymns came in the same manner.

One day someone was talking about wealth and said, "If I had wealth I would be able to do just what I wish to do; and I would be able to make an appearance in the world."

"Take the world, but give me Jesus!" Fanny Crosby replied, and wrote a hymn bearing that title. John R. Sweney set it to music:

> Take the world, but give me Jesus—
>   All its joys are but a name;
>   But His love abideth ever,
> Through eternal years the same.
>
> O the height and depth of mercy,
> O the length and breadth of love.
> O the fullness of redemption,
>   Pledge of endless life above.
>
> Take the world but give me Jesus,
>   Sweetest comfort of my soul;
> With my Saviour watching o'er me
>   I can sing, though billows roll.
>
> Take the world, but give me Jesus,
>   Let me view His constant smile;

Then throughout my pilgrim journey
Light will cheer me all the while.

Take the world, but give me Jesus:
In His cross my trust shall be,
Till, with clearer, brighter vision,
Face to Face my Lord I see.

While attending a prayer meeting Fanny found the people slow in standing and giving their personal testimonies. Feeling that Christians should be eager to witness, Fanny went home that night and wrote a hymn entitled "Just a Word for Jesus." W. H. Doane wrote the music for it. The song contains five verses, the first verse and chorus being:

Now just a word for Jesus;
Your dearest friend so true,
Come, cheer our hearts and tell us
What He has done for you.

Now just a word for Jesus—
'Twill help us on our way;
One little word for Jesus,
O speak or sing or pray.

Dr. Robert Lowry once asked Fanny to write a hymn on the subject, "The Bright Forever." For two days Fanny tried to write the hymn, but nothing came of her efforts. Then the words came suddenly in almost complete stanzas—faster than she could write them down.

W. H. Doane wrote the music for a beautiful hymn that is still used today and Fanny Crosby wrote the words. The verses and the chorus state:

To the work! To the work! We are servants of God
Let us follow the path that our Master has trod;
With the balm of his counsel our strength to renew,
Let us do with our might what our hands find to do.

To the work! To the work! Pressing on to the end,

> For the harvest will come, and the reapers descend;
> And the home of the Ransomed our dwelling will be,
> And our chorus for ever, "Salvation is free!"
>
> Toiling on, toiling on,
> Toiling on, toiling on,
> Let us hope, Let us watch,
> And labor till the Master comes.

One evening Fanny Crosby was speaking before a group of men in a New York mission. About midway in her message it became evident that she was confused in a statement she was attempting to make. She faltered and finally paused in her speech. Haltingly, she tried from the beginning of the statement, but again she failed. This was unusual for the blind woman, for normally she had no problems of this nature. At last she interrupted her planned remarks:

"It seems there is a young lad present tonight who has forsaken the things of God and the teachings of his parents," she said. "Would that young man see me after the meeting tonight. There is something I'd like to say to him."

Then Fanny was able to resume her message and concluded it without another hitch. At the close of the service, a boy of about eighteen came to her.

"I am the fellow you mentioned," he said, and Fanny spoke with him briefly. The two then knelt and when they rose to their feet, joy was evident on the young man's face.

"Now I can meet my mother in heaven, for I have found her God!" he said.

Fanny returned to her room that night and wrote:

> Rescue the perishing, Care for the dying,
> Snatch them in pity from sin and the grave;
> Weep o'er the erring one, lift up the fallen;
> Tell them of Jesus, the mighty to save.
>
> Rescue the perishing, care for the dying,
> Jesus is merciful, Jesus will save.

Hymns flowed from Fanny's pen. In spite of some of her work being stored for future use, her name was appearing in some of the hymnals more times than any other writer and sometimes, perhaps, as many times as several of the other authors combined. Her publishers and the men who set her hymns to music decided she should adopt some noms de plume. Whatever their reasons may have been, no one knows today. It may have been for commercial reasons. Perhaps they felt their hymnals would enjoy a greater sale if it appeared that more authors were involved. It may have been because she wrote so many that a number were written on the same subject or theme and they preferred more than one by-line. It may have been for any number of reasons, but whatever prompted the practice it is almost certain that Fanny Crosby had no objection, for she wrote for neither fortune nor fame, but for the glory of her Lord.

Besides her pen names, many of her hymns were published under a wide assortment of initials, such as F. J. C., F. C., F. J. V. A., and many others. Even her own name was given in varied forms, such as Fanny Crosby, F. Crosby, F. J. Crosby, Mrs. Van Alstyne, Mrs. Alexander Van Alstyne, Fanny Van Alstyne, and sometimes simply Fanny or Fannie.

Evidently some of her noms de plume were names of real people, probably as a gesture of love or friendship. Some of them were apparently names of nephews and nieces. Others were names of musicians she knew.

Fanny said of the practice:

A large number of my hymns have gone out into the world bearing noms de plume; and hundreds are yet to be set to notes, but enough have already been published to make me wish to avoid so many credits for authorship; hence the long list of pseudonymns I have adopted. According to Mr. Hubert P. Main, who collected them all, this list reached almost the hundred mark. [Others have estimated the number reached two hundred and more.]

Following is a partial list of pen names Fanny used:

Mrs. A. E. Andrews	James Eliott	Sam Martin
James Apple	Rian A. Dykes	Maud Marion
Rose Atherton	Grace J. Frances	Laura Miller
James Black	Victoria Frances	Alice Monteith
Henrietta E. Blair	Jennie Garnet	Sally Smith
Florence Booth	Jenie Glen	Sam Smith
Charles Bruce	Frank Gould	Victoria Stewart
Robert Bruce	Mrs. Kate Grinley	Victoria Sterling
Charles Burns	Ruth Harmon	Rian J. Sterling
Mary Carleton	Frances Hope	Julia Sterling
Leah Carlton	Myra Judson	Zemira Wallace
Lyman Cuyler	Martha J. Lankton	Mrs. C. M. Wilson
Ella Dale	W. Robert Lindsay	Carrie M. Wilson
Lizzie Edwards	Sally Martin	

How many hymns did Fanny Crosby write? For obvious reasons, no one knows for sure. In her autobiography written in 1903, twelve years prior to her death, she gave what apparently was a conservative estimate of "over five thousand." In 1906 she confessed the number may have reached "eight thousand." Others have made a study since her death and have agreed that Fanny Crosby probably wrote more than eight thousand published poems and hymns!

24
Top Thirty

Fanny Crosby wrote the words to thousands of hymns, and each of these, no doubt, has blessed many people throughout the world. To arbitrarily list her ten most popular hymns would be difficult and probably not 100 percent accurate. Many things would have to be considered, such as: the number of times the hymn has been published, sung, and heard; the number of copies that have been sold, the number of foreign languages the hymn has been translated into; the extent to which people have been blessed by it; the number of souls that have been saved on hearing it; and how the hymn has survived the times. Therefore, I am not in a position to name ten of her hymns and say, "These are her top ten."

If such a list were attempted, almost every reader would likely suggest at least one or two favorites he feels should be included—and he would have the same right to do so as I have. So, rather than list ten, I have listed the top thirty, and will leave the list incomplete. Each reader can then complete the list with his own favorites.

Among Fanny Crosby's thirty most popular hymns, the following titles almost certainly would appear. This list is not in any particular order, except for the first one and that is the one Fanny Crosby claimed as her favorite of all she wrote: Safe in the Arms of Jesus; Pass Me Not, O Gentle Saviour; Rescue the Perishing; Saved by Grace; Blessed Assurance; Praise Him! Praise Him!; Jesus Is Calling; 'Tis the Blessed Hour of Prayer; Near the Cross; Nearer the Cross; I Am Thine, O Lord (Draw Me Nearer); He Hideth My Soul; Will Jesus Find Us Watching; Close to Thee; Though Your Sins Be as

Scarlet; Redeemed.

Here are the words to a few of the hymns, some in part, others in their entirety:

Safe in the Arms of Jesus

Safe in the arms of Jesus,
Safe on His gentle breast,
There by His love o'ershaded,
Sweetly my soul shall rest.
Hark! 'tis the voice of angels
Borne in a song to me,
Over the fields of glory,
Over the jasper sea.

Safe in the arms of Jesus,
Safe from corroding care,
Safe from the world's temptations,
Sin cannot harm me there.
Free from the blight of sorrow,
Free from my doubts and fears;
Only a few more trials,
Only a few more tears!

Jesus, my heart's dear refuge,
Jesus has died for me;
Firm on the Rock of Ages
Ever my trust shall be.
Here let me wait with patience,
Wait till the night is o'er:
Wait till I see the morning
Break on the golden shore.

Chorus: Safe in the arms of Jesus,
Safe on His gentle breast,
There by His love o'ershaded,
Sweetly my soul shall rest.

Jesus Is Calling

Jesus is tenderly calling thee home,
Calling today, calling today;

Why from the sunshine of love wilt thou roam
Farther and farther away?

Jesus is pleading; O list to His voice:
Hear Him today, hear Him today:
They who believe on His name shall rejoice;
Quickly arise and away.

Chorus: Calling today, calling today,
Jesus is calling,
Is tenderly calling today.

Though Your Sins Be as Scarlet

Tho' your sins be as scarlet,
They shall be as white as snow:
Tho' your sins be as scarlet,
They shall be as white as snow.
Tho' they be red like crimson,
They shall be as wool!
Tho' your sins be as scarlet,
Tho' your sins be as scarlet,
They shall be as white as snow,
They shall be as white as snow.
He'll forgive your transgressions,
And remember them no more:
He'll forgive your transgressions,
And remember them no more;
"Look unto Me, ye people,"
Saith the Lord your God!
He'll forgive your transgressions,
He'll forgive your transgressions
He'll forgive your transgressions,
And remember them no more,
And remember them no more.

Saved by Grace

Some day the silver cord will break,
And I no more as now shall sing;
But, O the joy when I shall wake
Within the palace of the King!

Some day my earthly house will fall;
I cannot tell how soon 'twill be;
But this I know—my All in All
Has now a place in Heaven for me.

Some day, when fades the golden sun
Beneath the rosy-tinted west,
My blessed Lord will say, "Well done!"
And I shall enter into rest.

Some day,—till then I'll watch and wait,
My lamp all trimmed and burning bright,
That when my Saviour ope's the gate,
My soul to Him may wing its flight.

Chorus: And I shall see Him face to face,
And tell the story—Saved by Grace.
And I shall see Him face to face,
And tell the story—Saved by Grace.

Redeemed

Redeemed—how I love to proclaim it!
Redeemed by the blood of the Lamb;
Redeemed thro' His infinite mercy,
His child, and forever, I am.

Redeemed and so happy in Jesus,
No language my rapture can tell;
I know that the light of His presence
With me doth continually dwell.

I think of my blessed Redeemer,
I think of Him all the day long;
I sing for I cannot be silent;
His love is the theme of my song.

I know I shall see in His beauty
The King in whose law I delight;
Who lovingly guardeth my footsteps,
And giveth me songs in the night.

Chorus: Redeemed, redeemed,
Redeemed by the blood of the Lamb;
Redeemed, redeemed,
His child, and forever, I am.

'Tis the Blessed Hour of Prayer

'Tis the blessed hour of prayer, when our hearts lowly bend,
And we gather to Jesus, our Saviour and Friend;
If we come to Him in faith, His protection to share,
What a balm for the weary! O how sweet to be there!

'Tis the blessed hour of prayer, when the Saviour draws near,
With a tender compassion His children to hear;
When He tells us we may cast at His feet every care,
What a balm for the weary! O how sweet to be there!

'Tis the blessed hour of prayer, when the tempted and tried
To the Saviour who loves them their sorrow confide;
With a sympathizing heart He removes every care;
What a balm for the weary! O how sweet to be there!

Chorus: Blessed hour of prayer, blessed hour of prayer!
What a balm for the weary! O how sweet to be there!

He Hideth My Soul

A wonderful Saviour is Jesus my Lord,
A wonderful Saviour to me,
He hideth my soul in the cleft of the rock,
Where rivers of pleasure I see.

A wonderful Saviour is Jesus my Lord,
He taketh my burden away,
He holdeth me up, and I shall not be moved,
He giveth me strength as my day.

With numberless blessings each moment He crowns,
And filled with His fullness divine,
I sing in my rapture, oh, glory to God
For such a Redeemer as mine!

When clothed in His brightness, transported I rise
To meet Him in clouds of the sky,
His perfect salvation, His wonderful love,
I'll shout with the millions on high.

Chorus: He hideth my soul in the cleft of the rock
That shadows a dry, thirsty land;
He hideth my life in the depths of His love,
And covers me there with His hand,
And covers me there with His hand.

Blessed Assurance

Blessed assurance, Jesus is mine!
O what a foretaste of glory divine!
Heir of salvation, purchase of God,
Born of His Spirit, washed in His blood!

Perfect submission, perfect delight,
Visions of rapture now burst on my sight;
Angels descending bring from above
Echoes of mercy, whispers of love.

Perfect submission, all is at rest,
I in my Saviour am happy and blest,—
Watching and waiting, looking above,
Filled with His goodness, lost in His love.

Chorus: This is my story, this is my song,
Praising my Saviour all the day long.

25
Noms de Plume

It was revealed in previous chapters that much of Fanny Crosby's work has gone out under various pen names. A random sampling, with the name she used, is given here:

Hold Thou My Hand

Hold Thou my hand! so weak I am, and helpless
I dare not take one step without Thy aid;
Hold Thou my hand! for then, O loving Saviour,
No dread of ill shall make my soul afraid.

Hold Thou my hand! and closer draw me
To thy dear self, my hope, my joy, my all;
Hold thou my hand, lest haply I should wander,
And, missing Thee, my trembling feet should fall.

Hold Thou my hand! the way is dark before me
Without the sunlight of Thy face divine;
But when by faith I catch its radiant glory,
What heights of joy, what rapturous songs are mine.

Hold Thou my hand! that when I reach the margin
Of that lone river Thou didst cross for me,
A heavenly light may flash across its waters,
And every wave like crystal bright shall be.
—Grace J. Frances

I Must Have the Saviour With Me

I must have the Saviour with me,
For I dare not walk alone;

I must feel His presence near me,
And His arms around me thrown.

I must have the Saviour with me,
For my faith at best is weak;
He can whisper words of comfort
That no other voice can speak.

I must have the Saviour with me
In the onward march of life;
Through the tempest and the sunshine,
Through the battle and the strife.

Chorus: Then my soul shall fear no ill;
Let Him lead me where He will,
I will go without a murmer,
And His footsteps follow still.

—Lizzie Edwards

What Will You Do With Jesus?

What will you do with Jesus?
Think well e'er you decide;
Once came the fatal answer:
Let Him be crucified.
And will you slight His mercy,
And crucify again,
The Lord of life and glory,
For your redemption slain?

What will you do with Jesus?
He's knocking at your heart;
Will you admit the Saviour,
Or shall He now depart?
What will you say to Jesus?
Will you reject His love?
Can this vain world, so transient,
Give joy like that above?

—Julia Sterling

He Is Coming

He is coming, the "Man of Sorrows,"
Now exalted on high;
He is coming with loud hosannas,
In the clouds of the sky.

He is coming, our loving Saviour,
Blessed Lamb that was slain;
In the glory of God the Father,
On the earth He shall reign.

He shall gather His chosen people,
Who are called by His name;
And the ransomed of every nation,
For His own He shall claim.

Chorus: Hallelujah! Hallelujah!
He is coming again;
And with joy we shall gather round Him,
At His coming to reign.

—Alice Monteith

The Still Small Voice

In the silent watches of the night,
Came a still, small voice that said,
"Thorns and cross I bore for thee,
All thy sins on me were laid."

I will rest me, rest me ever there;
Blessed Saviour, Thou art mine;
In the calm and silent night,
I shall hear Thy voice divine.

Chorus: O my Saviour, I hear Thee still,
Gently calling me, Sweetly calling me
To the narrow, narrow way,
Leading on the endless day,
Where the blest have gone before.

—Ella Dale

Bring Them In

Christians, wake, no longer sleep;
Shall we rest while others weep?
Shall we sit with folded hands,
When the Lord Himself commands?

Do we love the Saviour's name?
Can our faith His promise claim?
Have we pledged to Him our all?
Shall we not obey His call?

There's a cross that we must bear
If the crown we hope to wear:
Onward then with vigor new;
Time is short, the days are few.

Chorus: Go and work! this hour begin;
Go and seek the lost to win
From the dark abodes of sin,
To the feast, O bring them in!

—Frances Hope

Oh Wondrous Name!

Oh, wondrous Name, by prophets heard
Long years before His birth;
They saw Him coming from afar,
The Prince of Peace on earth.

Oh, glorious Name the angels praise,
And ransomed saints adore,—
The Name above all other names,
Our Refuge evermore.

Chorus: The Wonderful! The Counsellor!
The Great and Mighty Lord!
The everlasting Prince of Peace!
The King, the Son of God!

—Victoria Frances

Is It Well With Thee?

Is it well with thee? Is it well with thee?
Hast thou felt the precious cleansing blood?
Art thou justified by a living faith?
Hast thou peace and fellowship with God?

Chorus: Is it well with thee? Is it well with thee?
Hast thou laid up thy treasure above?
With the eye of faith dost thou clearly see?
Is it well with thee? Is it well with thee?
—Mrs. F. J. V. A.

My Song Shall Be of Jesus

My song shall be of Jesus
His mercy crowns my days,
He fills my cup with blessings,
And tunes my heart to praise;
My song shall be of Jesus
The precious Lamb of God,
Who gave Himself my ransom,
And bought me with His blood.

My Song shall be of Jesus,
While pressing on my way
To reach the blissful region
Of pure and perfect day.
And when my soul shall enter
The Gate of Eden fair,
A song of praise to Jesus
I'll sing forever there.

—Mrs. Van Alstyne

Press On, Press On!

Press on, press on, with eager joy,
The Christian race to run:
Be strong in Him whose name you bear,
The Lord's anointed Son.

Let every weight be cast aside,
And each besetting sin,
With steadfast faith and firm resolve,
Press on the prize to win.

Press on, like those who safely now,
Among the host above;
Have reached the goal for which they sought,
And won their crowns of love.

Press on, press on, O glorious hope,
The time will not be long,
When you shall join the ransomed host,
And sing their victor song.

Chorus: Press boldly on at His command,
Whose word can never fail;
Since He, the world has overcome,
Thro' Him you shall prevail.

—Grace J. Frances

The Many Mansions

How oft our souls are lifted up,
When clouds are dark and drear,
For Jesus comes, and kindly speaks
These loving words of cheer.

How oft amid our daily toil,
With anxious care oppressed,
We hear again the precious word
That tells of joy and rest.

O may our faith in Him be strong,
Who feels our every care,
And will for us, as He hath said,
A place in heaven prepare.

Then let us work, and watch and pray,
Relying on the love
Of Him who now prepares a place
For us in heaven above.

Chorus: "In my Father's house are many mansions;
If it were not so I would have told you;
In my Father's house are many mansions,
I go to prepare a place for you."

—Charles Bruce

26
Fanny Crosby's Critics

Probably no one ever lived to adulthood and escaped criticism entirely. The more successful one is in his chosen field the more vulnerable, it sometimes seems, he is to such judgments. Although Fanny Crosby was loved and admired by untold thousands of people, she was not free from such attacks.

In earlier chapters of this book it was explained how her teachers attempted to discourage her poetic endeavors, and how the superintendent one time severely reprimanded her for allowing young Grover Cleveland to copy her poems during school hours. Throughout her life there were a number of other encounters.

Fanny Crosby was religiously patriotic, and she lived in an era when it was unthinkable for an American to speak out against his country or show disrespect to its flag. Apparently there was no middle ground, you were either a loyal American or you were disloyal.

Fanny kept a tiny silk American flag with her at all times and often displayed it on her dress. According to a newspaper report, Fanny entered a restaurant one day wearing this flag and sat at a table across from another woman. Evidently the presence of the flag displeased the woman greatly.

"Take that dirty rag away from here!" the woman demanded.

"Repeat that remark at your peril." Fanny said in no uncertain terms.

The manager, who knew Fanny, overheard the brief conversation. He came to the table and told the other woman to finish her meal, pay for it, and leave and never come again.

Thus, in this woman Fanny Crosby had at least one critic because of her staunch Americanism. And unless the newspaper reporter exaggerated the story, it seems the blind woman was ready to defend the flag as best she could.

When a writer is unknown, criticism is not a pleasant experience, but it generally is of a local nature and usually comes from another unknown, so it is not always taken seriously. On the other hand, when the writer becomes more successful and famous, normally his critics are better known and the criticism is more widely publicized through the news media. Some of it may be well-founded. Quite often it is prompted by envy. Other instances may be nothing more than the critic's desire to write his own story.

In his *English Hymns: Their Authors and History* (1886), S. A. W. Duffield wrote of Fanny Crosby Van Alstyne: "It is more to Mrs. Van Alstyne's credit as a writer that she has occasionally found a pearl than that she has brought to the surface so many oyster shells."

Shortly before his death, however, Dr. Duffield wrote to the publisher of his book, revising his statement: "I rather think her talent will stand beside that of Watts and Wesley, especially if we take into consideration the number of hymns she has written."

What perhaps was Fanny Crosby's most cruel and the least warranted criticism came from J. Julian in his *Dictionary of Hymnology* (1908). Mr. Julian wrote: "Notwithstanding the immense circulation thus given to Mrs. Van Alstyne's hymns, they are, with few exceptions, very weak and poor, their simplicity and earnestness being their redeeming features. Their popularity is largely due to the melodies to which they are wedded."

Although it is unlikely that he intended to, Mr. Julian may have touched on the qualities that have helped Fanny's hymns endure the years, "simplicity and earnestness." Are not these necessary in any good hymn? Do not these words describe the story of salvation itself?

On the whole, nevertheless, Fanny Crosby's critics have been few, and today her hymns still live. The *Guiness Book of World Records* lists her as the most prolific hymnist! Christians everywhere know her name and sing her hymns, but how many know the names J. Julian and S. A. W. Duffield?

> I know there's a rest that remaineth for me,
> A rest when my journey is o'er;
> I know that the ransomed in bliss I shall see,
> And labor and sorrow no more.
>
> Then onward I'll go, and with courage I'll tread
> The path my Redeemer has trod,
> Since He hath declared there remaineth a rest,
> A rest for the people of God.
>
> I know there's a rest that remaineth for me;
> I'll patiently wait till it come,—
> Till angels shall bear me away on their wings,
> And Jesus shall welcome me home.

27
Fanny's Other Writings

Fanny Crosby was a writer of fine hymns, and it was her hymns for which she was made famous. What is not commonly known is that she was also a prolific writer of secular poems, cantatas, popular songs, ballads, and fiction stories. For the most part, these were written prior to the writing of her first hymn in 1864.

In this chapter and the two to follow are some samples of her other writings.

Cora Bell

Where the brooklet from the hillside
Laughs and sparkles on its way,
And the downy crested robin
Trills and carols all the day,—
Where the springtime lingers longest,
And the summer loves to dwell,
Where the autumn fruits are sweetest,
Bloomed our darling Cora Bell.

Now among the roses hiding,
Now in merry childish glee,
Breathing strains our lips had taught her,
O, 'twas joy her form to see;
What a treasure heaven had lent us!
How we loved her none can tell;
Sweetest bud that ever blossomed
Was our darling Cora Bell.

Silent, voiceless, to our dwelling
Came a stranger wan and pale,

Laid his cold and icy fingers
On our lily of the vale;
While we watched her drooping, fading,
Over our hearts a sorrow fell,
And the zephyr, moaning, sighing,
Called in vain our Cora Bell.

Where the brooklet from the hillside
Wanders on its pretty way,
And the ringdove for its playmate
Sits and pines the long, long day,—
There we laid a broken casket,
But the soul we know full well
Through the gate of life has entered;
There we'll meet our Cora Bell.

Chorus: There was gladness in her footstep,
And her song was like a spell;
Every birdling in the valley
Knew the voice of Cora Bell.

The Violet's Answer

"Little violet, thou art lonely;
Wilt thou come and bloom with me?
All thy sister flowers have faded;
None are left to care for thee."
"No," she answered, "let me rather
In this quiet valley stay;
Near the graves of those I cherish
Let me live my life away,
Till I wither and decay."

Night and Morning

Lo, the vesper hour hath flown,
Voices of the dewy night
Hold me captive with delight
To their mystic tone.

Strangely wild, yet passing sweet,

Falls their music on my ear,
While a fountain soft and clear
    Murmers at my feet.

Ah, too soon the moments fly,
Now the bird his nest forsakes
And the rosy morning breaks
    From the Orient sky.

Sabbath Evening

Lo, the setting sun is stealing
Softly through the clustering vines;
On the spirit sweet peace sealing,
    As this Sabbath day declines.

Lovely spot, oh, sacred hour,
    Day of all our days the best,
Weakening the tempter's power,
    Pointing to the promised rest.

While we watch thy fading splendor,
    Thou adorner of the skies,
May we all our hearts surrender
    To the God who bade thee rise.

Thanksgiving Day

"They're coming home tomorrow night;
    A happy time 'twill be;"
The old man wiped his spectacles,
    And rubbed his hands with glee;
"We'll have the candles lighted,
    And burning in the hall;
They're coming home tomorrow night,
    The little ones and all.

"Now, Susie, don't be idle;
    There's heaps of work to do;
The pumpkin pies are yet to make
    The tarts and doughnuts, too;

Your limbs are young and supple,
And therefore you should be
As nimble as a cricket,
And busy as a bee.

"Poor grandma can't do everything,
For she is growing old;
And yet, for all, I tell you
She's worth your weight in gold.
There, grandpa was not scolding;
Don't cry, but run away;
They're coming home tomorrow night,
To spend Thanksgiving Day.

"I am too harsh with Susie;
I wish I was not so;
She always tries to please me,
And does her best, I know;
She left her home and parents,
And came with us to stay;
Well, she shall have a brand-new comb
To wear Thanksgiving Day.

"Ah, there she comes with grandma,
As chipper as a bird,
Her face all smiles and sunshine;
She has not told a word;
She never tells, but hides them
The cruel words I say;
But she'll not be the loser
On next Thanksgiving Day.

"They're coming home tomorrow night,
Ruth, Phoebe, Grace, and Ann,
Josiah, David, Benjamin,
Luke, Abel, Nate, and Dan,
Their children, wives, and husbands, too;
Some now are on their way;
They'll all be home tomorrow night,
To spend Thanksgiving Day.

"Our Dan is Susie's father;
A likely boy was he;

He married very early;
His wife was Patience Lee,
The finest girl in Springfield,
And well-to-do beside;
The Worcester folks turned out, I guess,
When Dan brought home his bride.

"Our children are not handsome,
But, like their mother, good;
She never spared the rod on them,
But trained them as she should;
They're every one a credit;
And proud am I to say,
They're coming home tomorrow night,
To spend Thanksgiving Day."

Up rose the stalwart farmer
Of threescore years and ten,
And one might almost fancy
He was growing young again;
He stepped around so quickly;
And oft was heard to say,
"They're coming home tomorrow night,
To spend Thanksgiving Day."

He walked about the farmyard,
Among the poultry there,
And looked to see that all were fed,
With more than usual care;
And then he met a neighbor,
And stopped him just to say,
"They'll all be home tomorrow night,
To spend Thanksgiving Day."

At length the morrow's morning
Broke cloudless and serene,
And Farmer Jones was early
A watcher of the scene;
His consort, too, had risen;
And Susie, glad and gay,
Called out, "Good morning, grandpa;
I'm just fifteen today."

"Then you shall have a present,"
Her grandpa smiling said;
"What shall I bring you, Daisy."
He stroked her glossy head;
She looked at him and answered,
Through tears that glistened bright,
"O love me just a little
When they all come home tonight."

And long before the shadows
Had gathered in the west,
The baking was completed,
The poultry killed and dressed;
The pretty comb was purchased,
And Susie heard to say,
"Dear grandpa, how I thank you;
You've cheered my heart today."

Soon wagon after wagon
Rolled up before the door;
The house was filled with music
And merriment once more;
The candles, too, were lighted,
And burning in the hall,
And Farmer Jones was shaking hands
With little ones and all.

The evening meal concluded,
The children snug in bed,
The older ones grew thoughtful,
And then a prayer was said;
And Farmer Jones with reverence
Did not forget to say,
"I praise Thee, Lord, that all are here,
To spend Thanksgiving Day."

And once again 'twas morning;
In health they all arose;
Beneath their own paternal roof
How tranquil their repose!
The day was soft and balmy,
And all to church had gone,

Except the little ones they left
To play upon the lawn.

The sermon was impressive,
It spoke of by-gone years;
And all the congregation
Were melted into tears—
Glad tears they were, and grateful
To Him who from above
Had blessed their yearly harvest,
And crowned it with His love.

A simple prayer was offered,
And then the Pastor came,
Shook hands with all so warmly,
And greeted each by name;
The poor were not forgotten,
Nor slighted by the way,
But shared his benediction
On that Thanksgiving Day.

Home went our friends delighted;
The hour was somewhat late;
The large old-fashoned table groaned
Beneath its heavy weight
Of poultry, pies, and puddings,
Of every name and kind,
And fragrant tea that so revives
And renovates the mind.

And thus the day wore onward,
Till all its joys were passed;
The stars came out at twilight,
The evening closed at last;
And, when to rest retiring,
They all were heard to say,
"God bless our dear New England
For such a glorious day."

Peace, Be Still

When, o'er the billows wild and dark
Was rudely tossed the Saviour's barque,

He calmed them by His sovereign will,
And bade the angry storm be still.

The wild winds cease—the billows sleep
In silence on the mighty deep;
For God, omnipotent to save,
Can calm the wind and rule the wave.

Thus when tempestuous passions swell,
And we against His law rebel,
O, may our hearts His Spirit fill,
And bid the angry storm be still.

And O, in sorrow's gloomy hour
Still may we own His sovereign power;
Bow meekly to His gracious will
And bid the throbbing heart be still.

The Hunter's Home

I love to watch these rugged hills,
By Hudson's rolling wave,
When angry clouds sweep o'er the sky,
And loud the tempests rave.

I love to climb the rocky steep,
Or in the silent glade
To wander forth in pensive thought,
When twilight shadows fade.

There fearlessly the wild deer bounds,
And blithely every morn,
The passing wind bears far away
The notes of the hunter's horn.

28
More of Fanny's Other Writings

Naturally some of Fanny Crosby's early writing was on the subject of blindness. Sometime prior to 1851 she wrote:

The Blind Girl's Song

They tell me of a sunny sky,
Tinged with ethereal light;
But, ah! for me, no sunbeams shine,
My day is veiled in night.

Yet, there's a beam, a nobler beam,
Of knowledge, bright and fair;
That beam may light my darkened path,
And soften every care.

The moon that o'er the sleeping earth
Shines forth in majesty,
The sparkling deep that proudly rolls,
Hath no delights for me.

Yet I can hear a brother's voice,
In tenderest accents speak;
And feel my gentle sister's tear,
Steal softly down my cheek.

Christians everywhere still love Fanny Crosby's hymns. Had we lived during the last century we could have enjoyed another type of song she wrote—the popular songs. The famous musician George F. Root set most of these to music. At least one of these is still used today. It is "There's Music in the Air." Although most publishers show Mr. Root's name on both sides of the page, as if he wrote both words and music, it was indeed Fanny Crosby who penned these words:

There's music in the air
When the infant morn is nigh,
And faint its blush is seen
On the bright and laughing sky;
Many a harp's ecstatic sound
Comes with thrill of joy profound,
While we list enchanted there
To the music in the air.

There's music in the air
When the noontide's sultry beam
Reflects a golden light
On the distant mountain stream;
When beneath some grateful shade
Sorrow's aching head is laid,
Sweetly to the spirit there
Comes the music in the air.

There's music in the air
When the twilight's gentle sigh
Is lost on evening's breast
As its pensive beauties die;
Then, O then, the loved ones gone
Wake the pure celestial song;
Angel voices greet us there
In the music in the air.

Another of Fanny's songs in the popular field is "The Hazel Dell":

In the Hazel Dell my Nelly's sleeping,
Nelly loved so long!
And my lonely, lonely watch I'm keeping,
Nelly lost and gone;
Here in moonlight often we have wandered
Through the silent shade;
Now where leafy trees and drooping downward
Little Nelly's laid.

In the Hazel Dell my Nelly's sleeping,
Where the flowers wave,
And the silent stars are nightly weeping
O'er poor Nelly's grave;
Hopes that once my bosom fondly cherished
Smile no more on me;
Every dream of joy, alas, has perished,
Nelly dear, with thee.

Now I'm weary, friendless and forsaken,
Watching here alone;
Nelly, thou no more wilt fondly cheer me
With thy loving tone;
Yet forever shall thy gentle image
In my memory dwell,
And my tears thy lonely grave shall moisten;
Nelly dear, farewell.

Chorus: All alone my watch I'm keeping
In the Hazel Dell,
For my darling Nelly's near me sleeping,—
Nelly dear, farewell.

In the Ozark region of Arkansas and Missouri, the Appalachian Mountains of Kentucky, and probably other areas, the people still cherish some of the ballad-type sacred songs. Some of the smaller churches may not be able to afford a piano or organ, but there is usually someone around who can play the guitar or autoharp by ear if not by note. Even the country music and string band shows on the radio stations usually close their programs with a hymn or sacred song. One of these still occasionally heard was written by Fanny Crosby in 1878:

Mother's Good-bye

Sit down by the side of your mother, my boy;
You have only a moment, I know:
But you'll stay till I give you my parting advice;
'Tis all that I have to bestow:
You leave us to seek for employment, my boy;
By the world you have yet to be tried;

But in all the temptations and struggles you meet,
　　May your heart in the Saviour confide.

You'll find in your satchel a Bible, my boy:
　　'Tis the book of all others the best;
It will teach you to live, it will help you to die,
　　And lead to the gates of the blest;
I gave you to God in your cradle, my boy:
　　I have taught you the best that I knew;
And as long as His mercy permits me to live,
　　I shall never cease praying for you.

Your father is coming to bid you good-bye;
　　O, how lonely and sad we shall be!
But when far from the scenes of your childhood
　　　　and youth,
　　You'll think of your father and me;
I want you to feel every word I have said,
　　For it comes from the depths of my love;
And my boy, if we never behold you on earth,
　　Will you promise to meet us above?

Chorus: Hold fast to the right, hold fast to the right,
　　Wherever your footsteps may roam;
O forsake not the way of salvation, my boy,
That you learned from your mother at home.

A Song

O come, if thou art true to me,
　　If yet thou lov'st me well,
And meet me at our trysting place
　　Within the mossy dell;

Yes, meet me as when first we met
　　Beneath a summer sky,
Long, long before our lips had learned
　　That cruel word, good-bye.

There's not a rose on yonder bush,
　　Nor flower we used to twine;
The birds have left that rural spot;

Perhaps the fault is mine:
I know my looks were cold and stern,
A frown was on my brow;
But I regret that fatal hour;
Wilt thou forgive me now?

O come, and let us plight once more
The faith of other years,
And bathe each link of sacred love
In sweet repentant tears;
Yet not one shadow would I cast
Around thy peerless name;
Mine, mine the wrong; I'll bear it all,
And I deserve the blame.

Voice of the Night Wind

Voice of the night wind, mournfully stealing
Forth from the depths of thy dark ocean cave,
Shrieking in terror, wailing in pity,
Chanting a dirge o'er the mariner's grave,—
What art thou saying? eager, I listen,
Catching each note of thy tremulous moan,
While my worn spirit, pining with anguish,
Sighs for the friends that have left it alone.
Voice of the night wind, speak to me gently,
Tell of the days that were cloudless and bright;
Bring, if thou canst, the fond hopes I have cherished,
Clothe them in beauty and deck them with light;
Fitfully breathing thy desolate moan,
While my worn spirit, crushed and forsaken,
Weeps for the friends that have left it alone.

The Heart

The heart! the heart! O wound it not,
That fond yet fragile thing;
Whose tendrils, like the clustering vine,
Around thine own would cling.
Though sunny beams may o'er thee play,
And smiles thy lip may wreathe,

And tender blossoms, pure and white,
  Their dewy fragrance breathe,—

Thou canst not tell in after years,
  How dark thy fate may be;
Then spurn thou not the trusting heart
  That warmly beats for thee.

The heart! the heart! O crush it not;
  'Tis but a fragile thing;
An altered look, a chilling word,
  Might break its sweetest string.

When, one by one, thy treasured hopes
  Like withered leaves shall fall,
Then wilt thou mourn, alas, too late,
  What tears can n'er recall.

It seems that almost any thought that came to Fanny's mind could be turned into verse: God, flowers, trees, politics, patriotism, statesmen, birth, death, birthdays, sadness, joy, love, and so on. A verse of one of her love poems called "Bid Me Good Night" says:

Bid me good night with a smile that will say
More than the language can ever portray;
Then let me carry that smile in my heart,
Changed to a pearl by love's magical art;
Come, for the moments are speeding their flight:
Bid me good night, darling, bid me good night.

Fanny received little or no income from many of the hymns and poems she wrote. The money she did receive was often shared or given in its entirety to those who needed it more than she. At least one of her songs was an exception. It was a popular song written in 1855, and netted almost three thousand dollars in royalties! Here are the words:

Rosalie, the Prairie Flower

On the distant prairie, where the heather wild,
In its quiet beauty, lived and smiled,
Stands a little cottage, and a creeping vine
Loves around its porch to twine;
In that peaceful dwelling was a lovely child,
With her blue eyes beaming soft and mild,
And the wavy ringlets of her flaxen hair
Floating in the summer air.

On that distant prairie, when the days were long,
Tripping like a fairy, sweet her song,
With the sunny blossoms and the birds at play,
Beautiful and bright as they;
When the twilight shadows gathered in the west,
And the voice of nature sank to rest,
Like a cherub kneeling seemed the lovely child,
With her gentle eyes so mild.

Chorus: Fair as a lily, joyous and free,
Light of that prairie home was she;
Everyone who knew her felt the gentle power
Of Rosalie, the Prairie Flower.

But the summer faded, and a chilly blast
O'er that happy cottage swept at last;
When the autumn song-bird woke the dewy morn,
Little Prairie Flower was gone;
For the angels whispered softly in her ear,
"Child, thy Father calls thee; stay not here;"
And they gently bore her, robed in spotless white,
To their blissful home in light.

Chorus: Though we shall never look on her more,
Gone with the love and joy she bore,
Far away she's blooming in fadeless bower,
Sweet Rosalie, the Prairie Flower.

29
Still More of Fanny's Other Writings

The Blind Harper

They passed him by with hurried steps,—
A gay and busy throng;
They passed him by, nor paused to hear
The son of Erin's song.

The passing breeze his white locks swayed,
His eyes with age were dim;
The midday sun in splendor shone,
But not, alas! for him.

Far from his own green ocean isle,
Of home and friends bereft,
The old man leaned upon his harp,—
All that to him was left.

As o'er the strings his fingers strayed,
Sad tears were falling fast;
For, oh! their every tone but seemed
An echo of the past.

"Ah me!" he sighed, "what mean these tears?
I as a child am weak!"
Then buried in his shrivelled hand
His pale and care-worn cheek.

I saw they coldly passed him by,
That gay and busy throng;
But there was one who turned to hear
That son of Erin's song.

My heart with gentle pity moved,
She wiped a tear away,

As plaintive on her ear there fell
A simple melody.

"Dear isle of the ocean, how oft have I sported
Amid thy green hills and thy valleys so fair!
To the banks of the Shannon how oft have resorted,
And plucked the sweet daisy and green shamrock there!

"Oh! never again shall my wild harp awaken
Its soft-breathing numbers on Erin's bright shore;
The cot of my father, alas! is forsaken;
The home of my youth I'll revisit no more.

"Farewell, O my country! dear isle of the ocean;
I'm weary of life and I pine to be free:
When to Heaven I offer my latest devotion,
I will not forget to make mention of thee."

He ceased, and quickly to his side
That gentle maiden came;
Long had she gazed, and much she wished
To ask the stranger's name.

"Sire!" she said: the old man turned
His sightless eyes around;
For oh! to him a voice so kind
Seemed an unearthly sound.

"Sire! That thrilling lay had waked
My deepest sympathy:—
And hast thou not one kindered heart
To feel or care for thee?"

"No, lady; no! I am alone,
Far from my native shore;
And those who loved me dearly once
I live but to deplore.

"The morn I left that sunny isle
I never can forget;
My broken-hearted mother's kiss,
Lady, I feel it yet.

"And then, how wildly round my neck
My only sister clung!
And soon above her silent grave
The drooping willow hung!"

"O minstrel! I can hear no more,"
The weeping maiden said;
And mournfully the old man laid
His hand upon her head.

"Go, lady, go; and evermore
O may'st thou happy be!
An old man's blessing take, 'tis all
He can bestow on thee."

The spring returned, the sylvan choir
Awoke the silent glade;
And gently through the forest trees
The balmy zephyrs played;

But the poor minstrel they had laid
Within the grave's dark cell,
Far from the land that gave him birth
And those he loved so well.

On Hearing a Description of a Prairie

Oh! could I see as thou hast seen,
The garden of the west,
When Spring in all her loveliness
Fair nature's face has dressed.

The rolling prairie, vast and wild!
It hath a charm for me—
Its tall grass waving to the breeze,
Like billows on the sea.

Say, hast thou chased the bounding deer
When smiled the rosy morn?
Or hast thou listened to the sound
Of the merry hunter's horn?

Once could the noble redman call
That prairie wild his home;—
His cabin now in ruins laid,
He must an exile roam,

And thou at twilight's pensive hour,
Perchance hast seen him weep;—
Tread lightly o'er the hallowed spot,
For there his kindred sleep.

I envy not the opulent
His proud and lordly dome;
Far happier is the pioneer
Who seeks a prairie home;—

Where no discordant notes are heard,
But all is harmony;
Where soars aloft unfettered thought,
And the heart beats light and free.

A Revery

Am I sleeping, am I waking?—
Hath my spirit winged her flight
To some pure and blissful region,
Bathed in soft and silvery light?

Am I sleeping, am I waking?—
Whence these sounds that greet my ear?
Come they on the midnight zephyr,
Wafted from some distant sphere?

Minstrel! o'er my wild harp bending,
I would touch its chords for thee;
Yet its tones are but the echo
Of thine own sweet minstrelsy.

Thou hast well deserved the chaplet
Which for thee I proudly twine,
Laurels from Castalia's fountain
Well may grace a brow like thine.

The Past

Oh! give me back the past again,
    With all its hopes and fears;
    Or let me weep in solitude,
    O'er childhood's vanished years.

Oh! give me back my mountain home,
    The willow by the brook;
    The robin that so sweetly sang
    Within my favorite nook.

And give me what of all I prize,
    The long tried friends of yore;
    The welcome grasp, the kindly glance,
    What could I long for more?

Vain wish! the past alone returns
    To memory's silent call;
Where nourished by the springs of thought,
    Our brightest treasures dwell.

I strive to mourn not for the joys
    That were too pure to last;
    But oh! my spirit yearns to feel
    The sunshine of the past.

A Visit to a Fixed Star

'Twas night, and by a fountain side
    I stood and mused alone:
    Strange objects rose upon my sight
    That were to me unknown.

Mysterious forms fantastic moved,
    With slow and measured tread,
    Like shadows floating in the air,
    Or spectres from the dead.

A goblet from that fountain filled,
    How quickly did I drain!
For those who taste its cooling draught
    May live the past again.

Then suddenly a meteor glare
Flashed from the midnight sky;
'Twas gone,—and on immensity
Was riveted mine eye.

Borne upward by a power unseen,
In air I seemed to glide;
Onward—still onward—was my course:
A spirit was my guide.

We passed on never tiring wings
Through boundless realms of space,
Till lost amid those clustering stars
That here we scarce can trace.

Vast suns, with burning satellites,
Burst on my wondering eyes:
Bewildered by their dazzling light,
I gazed in mute surprise.

"Tell me, celestial one," I said,
"If thou mayest be addressed,
Are not the brilliant orbs I see
The dwellings of the blest?—

"Can we the utmost limits reach?—
The heights of space attain?"
"When ends eternity," he cried,
"And Heaven shall cease to reign."

He spoke, then pointed to a star,
That far beyond us lay;
And swifter than on lightning's wing
We thither bent our way.

In robes of passing loveliness
Was Nature there arrayed;
The air was fragrant with the breath
Of flowers that never fade.

"Spirit," I asked, "can aught of grief
These regions fair molest?

My pinions gladly would I fold
In this bright land to rest."

"Mortal," he answered, "thou must pass
The portals of the dead;
For sacred are these verdant fields,
Where only spirits tread."

He ceased; then waved me back to earth:
I saw, I heard no more.
I woke as from a pleasing dream;
The mystic spell was o'er.

Under a Cloud

When my heart was almost breaking
'Neath its heavy weight of care,
And the cross that lay before me
Seemed too great for me to bear, —

Came a voice that whispered gently,
"Why discouraged shouldst thou be?
Answer this, and answer truly,
Art thou faithful? lovest thou Me?"

And I answered, "O my Saviour,
In my weakness make me strong;
Lord, Thou knowest that I love Thee,
And Thy love shall be my song."

When I tried to work for Jesus,
And I pleaded at His throne
For the witness of the Spirit
That my heart was still His own, —
How I felt reproved and humbled
When again He said to me,
"Answer this, and answer truly,
Have I e'er forsaken thee?"

And I answered, "O my Saviour,
In my weakness make me strong;

Lord, Thou knowest that I love Thee,
And Thy love shall be my song."

Now I rest securely, calmly,
For I know that He is nigh;
Pain or sickness, if He send it—
Not a murmur, not a sigh;
Still I hear His voice repeating,
"Once I bore the cross for thee;
Answer truly; art thou willing
Now to bear thine own for Me?"

Still I answer, "O my Saviour,
In my weakness make me strong;
Lord, Thou knowest that I love Thee,
And Thy love shall be my song."

30
Fanny's Scrapbook

Fanny Crosby made warm, lifelong friendships with many people, notables and unknown persons alike. She kept and cherished their letters, poems, and words of tribute. Some of these keepsakes are copied here.

Frances Ridley Havergal, the famous hymn writer from England, sent the following:

A Seeing Heart
To "Fanny Crosby"

Sweet blind singer over the sea,
Tuneful and jubilant! how can it be
That the songs of gladness, which float so far,
As if they fell from the evening star,
Are the notes of one who never may see
"Visible music" of flower and tree,
Purple of mountain, or glitter of snow,
Ruby and gold of the sunset glow,
And never the light of a loving face?
Must not the world be a desolate place
For eyes that are sealed with the seal of years,
Eyes that are open only for tears?
How can she sing in the dark like this?
What is her fountain of light and bliss?

O, her heart can see, her heart can see!
And its sight is strong, and swift and free;
Never the ken of mortal eye
Could pierce so deep, and far, and high
As the eagle vision of hearts that dwell
In the lofty, sunlit citadel
Of Faith that overcomes the world,

With banners of Hope and Joy unfurled,
Garrisoned with God's perfect Peace,
Ringing with paeans that never cease,
Flooded with splendor bright and broad,
The glorious light of the Love of God.

Her heart can see, her heart can see!
Well may she sing so joyously!
For the King Himself, in His tender grace,
Hath shown her the brightness of His face;
And who shall pine for a glowworm light
When the sun goes forth in His radiant might?
She can read His law, as a shining chart,
For His finger hath written it on her heart;
She can read His love, for on all her way
His hand is writing it every day.
"Bright cloud" indeed must that darkness be,
Where "Jesus only" the heart can see.

Her heart can see! her heart can see,
Beyond the glooms and the mystery,
Glimpses of glory not far away,
Nearing and brightening day by day:
Golden crystal and emerald bow,
Luster of pearl and sapphire glow,
Sparkling river and healing tree,
Evergreen palms of victory,
Harp and crown and raiment white,
Holy and beautiful dwellers in light;
A throne, and One thereon, whose face
In the glory that glorious place.

Dear blind sister over the sea!
An English heart goes forth to thee.
We are linked by a cable of faith and song,
Flashing bright sympathy swift along;
One in the East and one in the West,
Singing for Him whom our souls love best,
"Singing for Jesus," telling His love
All the way to our home above,
Where the severing sea, with its restless tide,
Never shall hinder, and never divide.

Sister! what will our meeting be,
When our hearts shall sing and our eyes shall see!

To Fanny
By Robert Lowry

The sun of life will darken,
The voice of song will cease,
The ear to silence harken,
The soul lie down in peace,—
But with the trumpet's sounding,
Ten thousand suns will glow,
And endless hymns abounding
Like streams of love will flow.

Many of Fanny's friends and associates sent her a poem each year on her birthday. In contrast to the one above, Hubert P. Main usually sent a humorous one:

O Fanny, you're the worstest one,
As ever yet I've knew,
You ask for things inopportune,
You du, you know you du!
It's every year along in March,
When tree toads 'gin to roam,
You set me wilder than a hawk
A howlin' for a *pome.*

I'm pestered, bothered, sick to death,
I have so much tu du
On books, and services, and sich:—
I hev no time for you.

Still March the twenty-four comes round;
In spite of earth or heaven;
And you keep coming also, tew,
For now you're seventy-seven.

Lord bless you, Fanny; this I'll say
Since while my mill is runnin',
I'm in dead earnest, too, and pray
You will not think me funnin'."

In the summer of 1900, Ira D. Sankey was engaged in an evangelistic tour in England. He wrote:

Dear Fanny:

You are not forgotten and your name is often mentioned in connection with "Saved by Grace" in my services. We are keeping well and are just starting for Leeds, York, Sunderland, Berwick, Newcastle, and Edinburgh, where large halls have been taken for our meetings. I quoted your beautiful lines of poetry recently in Birmingham:

> Oh, for an angel's harp to tell
> How much I love Thee and how well!

They are fine and some of our mutual friends have written them down in their Bibles. I hope you are still as bright as a dollar, as you say.

Sincerely yours,
Ira D. Sankey

On Fanny's eighty-fifth birthday, Grover Cleveland wrote:

My dear friend:

It is more than fifty years ago that our acquaintance and friendship began; and ever since that time I have watched your continuous and interested labor in uplifting humanity, and pointing out the way to an appreciation of God's goodness and mercy.

Though these labors have, I know, brought you abundant rewards in your consciousness of good accomplished, those who have known of your works and sympathized with your noble purposes owe it to themselves that you are apprized of their remembrance of these things. I am, therefore, exceedingly gratified to learn that your eighty-fifth birthday is to be celebrated with a demonstration of this remembrance. As one proud to call you an old friend, I desire to be early in congratulating you on your long life of usefulness, and wishing you in the years yet to be added to you, the peace and comfort born of the love of God.

Yours very sincerely,
Grover Cleveland

Miss Eliza E. Hewitt, also a writer of many fine hymns, wrote a tribute to Fanny Crosby in 1905:

> The friends are forming a garland,
> Fragrant and lovely and sweet,
> The roses and lilacs of friendship,
> To lay at our loved one's feet;
>
> And while the fair chaplet they're twining,
> May I bring a little flower,
> A forget-me-not, meek and lowly,
> To add to the joys of the hour?
>
> This love-wreath is for our dear "Fanny,"
> Whose heart is so young and so true,
> No wonder her songs, freely gushing,
> Are as fresh as the morning dew!
>
> They sparkle with Spring's happy sunshine,
> They ripple like streams of delight,
> They flow from the rocks of the mountain,
> They touch us with love's tender might.
>
> Because she sings of her Saviour,
> And His spirit tunes her lyre,
> Her work shall go on forever,
> And she has been called up higher.
>
> So we'll gather round our "Fanny,"
> With smiles and greetings sincere;
> May she have just the sweetest birthday
> She has had for many a year.
>
> Then we'll all be happy with her,
> And thank the dear Lord above,
> For sending us one of His angels
> To sing to us of His love.

And on March 24, 1893, Ira D. Sankey wrote:

O friend beloved, with joy again
We hail thy natal day,
Which brings you one year nearer home,
Rejoicing on the way.

How fast the years are rolling on—
We cannot stay their flight;
The summer sun is going down,
And soon will come the night.

But you, dear friend, need fear no ill;
Your path shines bright and clear;
You know the Way, the Truth, the Life,
To you He's ever near.

And when you pass from time away
To meet your Lord and King,
In heaven you'll meet ten thousand souls,
That you have taught to sing.

A few more years to sing the song
Of our Redeemer's love;
Then by His grace both you and I
Shall sing His praise above.

In 1903 Margaret E. Sangster, talented song writer and poet in her own right, wrote:

The dear Lord has kept her close to Him,
In a little curtained space
That never is wholly dusk or dim,
Because of His shining face;
Though we are afraid of the brooding dark
It cannot be so to her,
For the Lord Himself has made an ark
For His loving worshipper.

There are things of earth that she cannot see,
Except with her spirit's eyes;

The light in the blossom-perfumed tree,
The stars in the still night-skies;
But never imagine she has not known
Far fairer sights than ours!
The hem of His garment round her thrown
Is broidered with fadeless flowers.

She smiles the smile of a happy child,
Her voice as the child's is sweet,
She has followed so safe through wood and wild,
The print of her Saviour's feet.
Her ear, attuned to the finest chord,
Has caught the songs of heaven;
She has taught us all how to praise her Lord
For the grace of sins forgiven.

Her song has bubbled with notes of joy,
Has risen in faith so strong,
It has reached the height where the whole employ
Is praise, where the ransomed throng.
And year by year as the sifted snow
Of age on her head is white,
She has been as a child of the long ago,
In her dear Lord's loving sight.

Why call her blind, who can see so well
The hidden things and clear:
Who knows so much that she may not tell,
Of the land that's drawing near?
The pure in heart, our Saviour said,
And the word is true for aye,
Though drifting centuries on have sped,
Since He went to His home on high.

The pure in heart shall *see*, ah! yes,
They shall see the face of Him
Who dwells forever in ceaseless bliss
Between the cherubim.
Of her we love, this wondrous word
Is true in very deed.
'Tis the sight of her own, her loving Lord,
In her sightless eyes we read.

God bless her ever! we lift the prayer—
Our hearts would hold her fain
To guard her now from the weight of care,
To shield her life from pain.
And when at last an angel comes
To lead her in to the King,
God give her a place in the best of homes
Where the choiring angels sing!

May the thin veil drop from the gentle eyes,
And by the King's own grace
When she sees Him, clear, with no surprise,
May she have a sheltered place
In a little corner white and fair,
And very near His feet:
And never a voice 'mid the voices there,
Shall ring more true and sweet!

31
Missions, YMCA's and the Salvation Army

George M. Brown, pastor of the First Methodist Episcopal Church in Bridgeport, Connecticut, where Fanny Crosby was a member, said of her:

"Her hymns have won thousands to penitential tears. And it is not to be wondered at, for she believed that no man sank so low but that he could be reclaimed by salvation."

The lines Fanny wrote seem to substantiate Dr. Brown's statement: "Rescue the Perishing," "Pass Me Not," and "Though Your Sins Be as Scarlet," for examples.

Though your sins be as scarlet,
They shall be as white as snow,
Though they be red like crimson,
They shall be as wool!

The Reverend Albert G. Ruliffson founded the famous Bowery Mission in 1879. Although Fanny Crosby was active in several New York missions, she probably spent more time at this one than any other, for she and Mr. and Mrs. Ruliffson were close, personal friends. Some of her famous hymns were written in connection with her experiences at these missions, such as "Rescue the Perishing," the story of which was related in a previous chapter.

Once Fanny said:

Kindness in this world will do much to help others, not only to come into the light but to grow in grace day by day. There are many timid souls whom we jostle morning and evening as we pass them by; but if only the kind word were spoken they might become fully persuaded. For all mission workers everywhere I always have had tender sympathies. God bless them!

I could give more than one instance where men have been reclaimed, after a long struggle and many attempts at reformation, because someone spoke a kind word to them even at what appeared to be the last moment. I have also known many others who turned away from a meeting simply because the cheering word had not been spoken, nor the helping hand extended.

Never to chide the erring has always been my policy, for I firmly believe that harsh words only serve to harden hearts that might otherwise be softened into repentance.

> Speak not harshly when reproving
> Those from duty's path who stray;
> If we would reclaim the erring,
> Kindness must each action sway.
>
> Speak not harshly to the wayward;—
> Win their confidence—their love;
> They will feel how pure the motive
> That hath led us to reprove.
>
> Speak not harshly to the stranger,
> Though he comes in humble guise;
> Think how slight a thing would kindle
> Gladness in a stranger's eyes.
>
> Speak not harshly to the felon,
> Though like adamant his heart;
> Touch one chord of fond affection,
> And the scalding tear may start.
>
> Speak not harshly to the orphan,
> He has borne of grief his share;
> Add not to his heavy burden,
> Add not to corroding care.
>
> Speak not harshly, was the precept

Which to man the Saviour taught;—
May that precept ever guide us—
Gentle words will cost us naught.

At the peak of Fanny Crosby's activity among the missions, railroads and trolleys had become the chief means of transportation within and between the cities in the United States. These industries employed a large number of men, especially in the larger cities, such as New York. Fanny was already active in the regular branches of Young Men's Christian Associations, and when "railroad" branches started forming, she was thrilled.

"Railroad men are my boys," she said. "I love every one of them . . . . Many and many a time I have spoken for them in their YMCA meetings and in their missions, and it has always cheered my heart when I have heard those strong men sing some of the hymns I have written."

There is no doubt but that Fanny was pleased that these men now had a special place to stay. Her greatest joy, I'm sure, came from knowing that they would be exposed to a Christian atmosphere. It was the only such contact that many of them had.

Fanny's talent and habit of expressing vast numbers of her messages in verse did not leave her boys out. One Christmas she wrote to them:

How I would like to shake your hands,
And greet you one by one;
But we are now too far apart,
And this cannot be done.

Yet I can hope, and wish, and pray
That Heaven's eternal joys
May fall like dew upon your heads,
My noble railroad boys.

Fanny loved the Salvation Army, and often took part in their meetings. She related the following story to a minister friend, S. Trevena Jackson, and he quoted it in his *Fanny Crosby's Story of Ninety-Four Years:*

I suppose you are curious to know how I happened to visit Cambridge. Well, over thirty years ago I met a young Baptist preacher who was very much concerned in my work among the railroad men and among the outcast. His name was Campbell. He was a sturdy Scotch Canadian. I felt that he had in him great possibilities, and soon he was called to a large church in this educational center. You know a clergyman must continue to climb if he is to hold his own in the shadow of old Harvard. This he has done. For years I had lost sight of him, but now through some dear friends the door was thrown wide open for my visit. It had always been one of the great desires of my heart to visit Harvard and come if only for a brief space under the influence of that haunt of literary and educational power.

A drizzling cold rain, which would have chilled many at my age, was falling but that did not discourage me in the least. We started with a song, "What Care I for Time or Tide." On the way to Boston I had four hours of the sweetest expectation possible. On reaching Back Bay Station, a taxi met us and the good Scotch minister took me up in his arms and landed me safely in a cushion seat, and before I could say 'Jack Robinson' I was at 300 Magazine Street, Cambridge.

Just as the evening meal was over, the doorbell rang, and a delegation from The Salvation Army entered with a request they be permitted to accompany me to the church (where I was to speak) with a brass band and play some of my hymns. The request was readily granted and so the next evening they came with their instruments and played many of my songs in front of the manse. Then followed by hundreds of people I marched from the house to the church, to the music of "Rescue The Perishing." They told me that more than two thousand people were present. I spoke to

them from my very heart of that wonderful story of Jesus
Christ who came into this world with a love big enough to
fill every nook and corner of it, if only mankind would allow
Him. It was a great service, the presence of Christ being
felt both in the music and the message.

At the age of eighty-six Fanny Crosby wrote a special hymn
befitting the Salvation Army, or of any other group of Christian soldiers. The title is "The Blood-Washed Throng," and it
is one of the few hymns for which she composed both words
and music:

> There is a blood-washed multitude,
> A mighty army strong;
> The Lord of hosts their righteousness,
> Redeeming love their song.
> They follow Christ whose name they bear,
> To yonder portals bright,
> Where He has said His faithful ones
> Shall walk with Him in white.
>
> That precious name their guiding star,
> Its beams will o'er them cast,
> And through its power their trusting souls,
> Shall overcome at last.
> The glory-cloud will bring them safe
> To yonder palace bright,
> Where they shall see Him eye to eye
> And walk with Him in white.
>
> March on! O blood-washed multitude,
> For lo! the hour draws nigh,
> When we shall hail the King of kings
> Triumphant in the sky,
> When songs of praise to Him we love,
> Shall fill the courts of light,
> And they that overcome the world,
> Shall walk with Him in white.

Near the turn of the century there appeared a man proclaiming himself to be "the Christ," an occurrence that still happens even today. This man went about the city, speaking on street corners and other places where he could attract a few listeners. Within a few weeks he had quite a following, and on one Sunday evening he chose a certain street corner on which to speak. What he was not aware of was that on the opposite corner the Salvation Army always held their Open Air Meetings. This group soon arrived and began singing and playing their instruments, completely oblivious of who the man on the other corner was or what he was doing. During the course of the meeting, according to the story as it was told to Fanny Crosby, the Salvation Army group sang one of her hymns:

> When my life-work is ended and I cross the swelling tide,
>   When the bright and glorious morning I shall see,
> I shall know my Redeemer when I reach the other side,
>   And His smile will be the first to welcome me.
>
>   I shall know Him, I shall know Him,
>   And redeemed by his side I shall stand
>   I shall know Him, I shall know Him
>   By the print of the nails in His hand.

It is said that one in the group listening to the man claiming to be Jesus shouted, "Look! There's no nail prints in *his* hands!" and the crowd slowly dispersed. The man, according to the story, disappeared from the scene and was never heard from again.

> Praise Him! praise Him! Jesus, our blessed Redeemer!
>   Sing, O earth—His wonderful love proclaim!
> Hail Him! hail Him! highest archangels in glory;
>   Strength and honor give to His holy name!
> Like a shepherd, Jesus will guard His children,
>   In His arms He carries them all day long;
> Praise Him! praise Him! tell of His excellent greatness,
>   Praise Him! praise Him! ever in joyful song!

32
Fanny Crosby at Carnegie Hall

In 1897 Fanny Crosby compiled her fourth book of poetry, and this one continued through at least five editions. Its title is *Bells at Evening and Other Verses,* and it contains an extensive biographical sketch by Robert Lowry.

The first poem in the book is "Bells at Evening":

> I turned from the crowded city,
> And strolled by myself alone,
> Languidly musing, and humming a tune
> In a dull and drowsy tone,
> Till I came to a lovely village
> That nestled among the dells:
> Then my heart leaped up with a strange,
> wild thrill
> At the sound of the evening bells,—
>
> Now bursting in sudden clangor,
> Now melting in softer strains,
> Till I felt the power of my soul entranced,
> Held fast by unyielding chains;
> E'en now I can hear the echo
> That floated among the dells;
> And I weep as then I wept for joy
> At the sound of the evening bells.
>
> Ah me, it is bright as ever,
> The close of a halcyon day
> That down in the vault of a mouldering past
> I thought I had laid away;
> But the same warm gush of feeling
> Again in my bosom swells;
> And I wonder if still from the old church spire
> Ring out those evening bells.

I think of that rustic village,
Secluded as once it stood,
With its dwellings so unpretending,
That sheltered the pure and good;
And a lone, sweet voice is blending
With the echoes among the dells;
And a form trips by with a fairy tread,
As I list to the evening bells.

I stand where a whitethorn blossoms,
But not by myself alone;
I am looking into a girlish face,
And catching her every tone;
And this is our young love's dawning;
What rapture its memory tells!
And our hearts keep time with the mellow chime,
The chime of the evening bells.

O throb of a passing moment!
O bliss that will come no more!
We met, and too soon we parted;
The dream of my life is o'er;
The bells of my heart are silent;
She sleeps in that distant clime;
But I sometimes ask if her soul can hear
The bells at the evening time.

The bells of my heart are silent,
The springs of my youth are dry;
And yet in my lonely musings
I long like a bird to fly;
I yearn for one look at the village
That nestles among the dells;
Then to pass away in the gloaming
'Mid the chiming of evening bells.

By the time she reached the height of her hymn writing career, Fanny Crosby's name was well known in Christian homes throughout the nation. The Moody-Sankey evangelistic team introduced and used most of her hymns in this country and in many foreign countries, especially England

and Scotland. Many of these hymns were translated into foreign languages—one newspaper report said *every* language.

Those who knew Fanny Crosby loved her. Those who did not know her personally but knew her hymns, were eager to meet her. She was widely sought after as a speaker for civic, patriotic, and religious meetings. Whether she was mingling with and witnessing to the outcast on skid row, telling stories to a group of children, or entertaining a president of the United States, Fanny Crosby was the same, unpretentious Christian lady. And those who knew her best affectionately called her "Aunt Fanny."

> I have heard the children singing
> When my heart was lone and sad;
> I have heard them in the distance
> And their music made me glad.
> But their voices cheer and charm me
> In the Sabbath homes they love;
> And I think they will be the sweetest
> In the saintly choirs above.

Typical of the headlines that appeared during Fanny Crosby's lifetime is this one that was carried in a Bridgeport, Connecticut, newspaper on September 17, 1910: "Blind Poetess Moves Veterans Almost to Tears." The article described how Fanny addressed a group of veterans and recited a poem written just for them.

During the summer of 1911, when Fanny Crosby was ninety-two years old, the following headlines appeared in a New York paper: "5,000 Sing With Blind Hymn Writer."

> Five thousand persons attended the opening rally of Evangelistic Committee's seventh annual, tent, open air, and shop campaign at Carnegie Hall last night. Massed on raised seats in the rear of the stage a choir of 200 voices made the big auditorium resound with hymns.

The feature of the exercises was the presence of Fanny Crosby, the venerable evangelist and hymn writer, who is now in her ninety-second year.

The newspaper related that the audience had joined the choir in singing for about half an hour before the addresses began. When blind Fanny Crosby made her way down the aisle and was assisted up the long flight of steps leading to the stage, the audience and choir began singing in a rousing manner one of Fanny's early compositions, "We Are Traveling On!"

Some in the audience commented on how frail and feeble Fanny looked as she was assisted up the steps, but when she was led to the front and center of the stage and began to speak, they changed their minds. With one hand resting on a chair back, her only support, she spoke in a loud, clear voice—after the applause had subsided enough for her to speak at all, that is.

"When I was taken from the carriage into the hotel today," she said, "I heard some one say: 'Get her a rolling chair.' But I spoke right out and said; 'I don't need any rolling chair. I can walk on my own feet. My strength is in the Lord!' "

It was reported that God wonderously blessed the meeting, and he did so, no doubt, because Fanny Crosby and others there lived the words she wrote:

> O Thou to whom, without reserve,
>   My all I would resign,
>   I ask for grace and faith to say,
>   "Thy will, O Lord, not mine!"
>   In joy or grief, in bliss or pain,
>   This prayer shall rise to Thee,
> "Thy will, not mine, O blessed Lord,
>   Thy will be done in me!"
>
> Though thorns may pierce my weary feet,
>   Yet would I ne'er repine,
>   But meekly say, as Thou hast said,

"Thy will, O Lord, not mine!"
And though I pass beneath Thy rod,
Amen, so let it be!
Whate'er Thou wilt, O blessed Lord,
I know is best for me.

So would I live that I may feel
Thy perfect peace divine,
And still Thy pure example show
In every act of mine;
And till I reach the silent vale,
And cross the narrow sea,
Be this my prayer, O blessed Lord,
"Thy will be done in me!"

33
Twilight

It was a bright October evening and the church was filled to overflowing, creating a scene typical of Fanny Crosby's speaking engagements.

"My dear, dear friends," Fanny said, "I am happy to greet you here tonight. These ninety years are rich with the wealth of goodness sparkling with the best spirit of sweetness and overflowing with the true wine of joy and gladness."

Fanny mentioned her "evening tide of life" and "living in the sight of eternity's sunrise." Although her speech was long and she was at an advanced age, she spoke with vigor and force. She gave proper credit to the source of her strength, and that strength was evident in the strong, steady voice she maintained throughout her message.

Hope seemed to be her dominant theme that night, for she told of how it had carried her through the years and how it increased as the years went by. Many of her songs and poems were written along these lines. "Hope On, Hope Ever" says in conclusion:

> Hope on, hope ever. Weary and oppressed,
> Care's pallid seal stamped on thy sunken cheek,
> There is a haven of eternal rest
> Whose sacred joy no mortal tongue can speak;
> Look upward in thine hour of dark despair—
> Hope points to heaven, and drops her anchor there.

On another occasion Fanny said, "I am often asked, 'Do you write as many hymns as ever?' Perhaps not quite: but this is owing to the fact that I spend so much time visiting churches in different parts of the country, and speaking, and reading my poems to audiences."

And Fanny was right. She was an industrious woman— always busy. If she was not speaking, she was visiting the sick, writing a letter of sympathy to a bereaved family, or writing a poem or hymn—right up to her last day on earth. Even while visiting or composing hymns and poetry she normally was occupied additionally, knitting a gift for her hostess or for someone else.

"The city of Bridgeport (Connecticut) has always had peculiar attractions for me." Fanny wrote in her autobiography in 1906. "Not only because it has long been the home of most of those who are near my heart by ties of blood, but because also of the delightful acquaintance of many of her generous citizens."

When Fanny was in her late seventies, her two sisters in Bridgeport urged her to give up her residence in New York and move in with one of them, or at least move near them. They reasoned that because she was blind and growing old, she needed their attention. Fanny refused to discuss the matter until in 1900 a serious illness caused her to reconsider. In May of that year she moved in with her widowed sister, Mrs. C. W. (Carrie) Rider, who had rooms in the home of a Mrs. Becker on State Street. Fanny lived there until June, 1907, when Carrie died.

Fanny's stepbrother, William Morris, had died in 1880, but one of his daughters, Mrs. Henry Booth, lived not far from the Becker house, at 226 Wells Street. Mrs. Florence Booth took the aging blind lady into her home. Fanny lived there her remaining years and Florence watched over her almost constantly. On some days when visitors came too frequently or when Fanny was unusually tired, Florence had the unpleasant task of turning people away at the door. She did so, of course, asking them to return when Aunt Fanny felt better.

From 1900 intil 1915, Fanny Crosby was active in the work

of the YMCA, Christian Endeavors, the Bridgeport Christian Union, Kings Daughters (later named "Fanny Crosby circle, Kings Daughters," in her honor), and she was instrumental in organizing the Traveler's Aid Society in Bridgeport. She worked with temperance groups and was a member of the First Methodist Episcopal Church.

Fanny often spoke in churches of various denominations, and she felt equally at ease in a fine church building in an affluent neighborhood, a mission house in a blighted area of the city, or in the Salvation Army Open Air meetings on a street corner.

Fanny Crosby never forgot the birthdays of her friends and relatives, and those days were joyous ones indeed. Her own birthdays, too, were times of celebration. As the years wore on with more and more of these days in the past and fewer to look forward to, they took on a deeper meaning still. It became a custom to celebrate her birthday-eve at church and the day itself at the office of the Biglow and Main Company, the company that published most of her hymns.

On one of her birthdays members of the church presented her with a "money tree," with a dollar attached for each of her years.

On the eve of her eighty-eighth birthday the Young People's Societies of the churches in Connecticut presented her with a watch, and this was one of Fanny's happiest birthdays, and to those present, it was perhaps the most touching. The Reverend G. M. Brown, pastor, had the honor of making the presentation. The blind lady was so overcome with joy and emotion, she was unable to speak to the audience and asked Mr. Brown to do so for her, "for if I do, I shall cry," she said.

When she had regained her composure, she said, "I would like to tell a secret; I've a chain about my neck and although I didn't know what it was for before, now I do. It must have been for that watch."

The watch was a repeater watch and was described in a

newspaper story:

> It is a plain, open faced, 18 karat minute repeating watch with a low chime for the hour, a high chime for the minutes, and both for quarters for the hour.
>
> When the little lever is pressed, the chimes strike the hour, the quarter hour and then the minutes any time when desired. If the lever is pressed at 25 minutes of ten, the low chime strikes nine times, the low and the high chime strikes five times for the minutes.

Monogrammed on the back of the watch were the letters, *F. J. C.* Inside the back was the following inscription: "1820 Presented to Fanny Crosby on her eighty-eighth birthday, by the Young People's Societies and other friends of Connecticut 1908."

The cost of the watch, incidentally, was $175.00, an expensive gift in 1908. Additional expense for the program brought the total to $219.83.

Did Fanny's Christian experience wane with the years? She answered that when she was ninety: "My love for the Holy Bible and its sacred truth is stronger and more precious to me at ninety than at nineteen." She used her Bible for the purpose she believed God intended it and had no time for those who wished to argue over the Scriptures for the sake of argument. She loved to claim its promises and did so every day. One of her hymns was entitled "Trust in the Promise," and it says in part:

> Brother, is your faith looking upward today?
> Trust in the promise of the Saviour;
> Sister, is the light shining bright on your way?
> Trust in the promise of the Lord.

After the death of Ira D. Sankey, his son wrote much of the music for Fanny's hymns. The son, I. Allan, compiled a collection of hymns in 1907, under the title *Hallowed Hymns,*

New and Old. This volume contained some of Fanny's older hymns and many of her more recent ones. It is interesting to note that many of these were still of the Christian soldier type, under such titles as "Girded for Battle," "Press On, Press On!" and "Gird on the Royal Armor." But perhaps even a larger number dwelled on Fanny's hope and anticipation of the new home to which she soon would be going. In 1896 she wrote "Almost in Sight of the Harbor," and it expressed hope and anticipation so prominent in many of her later hymns:

> Almost in sight of the harbor;
> O what a beautiful throng
> Over me lovingly bending,
> Singing a lullaby song!
>
> Almost in sight of the harbor;
> Perfect and peaceful my rest,
> Trusting my precious Redeemer,
> Sheltered and safe on His breast.
>
> Almost in sight of the harbor
> Surely my spirit has been;
> Yet, to the dear ones I cherish,
> Prayer has restored me again.
>
> *Chorus:* Almost in sight of the harbor,
> Almost at home on the shore;
> Only the signal to enter,
> Only a stroke of the oar.

34
In the Bright Forever

Breaking through the clouds that gather
O'er the Christian's natal skies,
Distant beams, like floods of glory,
Fill the soul with glad surprise;
And we almost hear the echo
Of the pure and holy throng,
In the bright, the bright forever,
In the summerland of song.

Yet a little while we linger,
Ere we reach our journey's end;
Yet a little while of labor,
Ere the evening shades descend;
Then we'll lay us down to slumber,
But the night will soon be o'er;
In the bright, the bright forever,
We shall slumber nevermore.

O the bliss of life eternal!
O the long, unbroken rest
In the golden fields of pleasure,
In the region of the blest!

But to see our dear Redeemer,
And before His throne to fall,
There to hear His gracious welcome,
Will be sweeter far than all.

Chorus: On the banks beyond the river,
We shall meet, no more to sever,
In the bright, the bright forever,
In the summerland of song.

It was Thursday night, February 11, 1915, and although the hour was late, a light still shone from a window at 226 Wells Street, Bridgeport, Connecticut. It was at that address Fanny Crosby lived and it was in her room that the light shone—not that she needed the light herself, but she wanted to dictate a message. Florence who took the message down needed the light to see as she wrote the following:

Thursday Evening

My dear, dear friends:

What shall I say? How shall I comfort you in this hour of your bereavement? I can scarcely realize that the white-robed angel has entered your home and left you desolate; yet no, you are not desolate, for there comes a message of inspiration that whispers to you all: "What I do ye know not now, but you shall know hereafter." And you know that your precious Ruth is "Safe in the arms of Jesus."

In 1884 Fanny had published a hymn called "Some Sweet Day, By and By." She adapted some of the words for the occasion that night and included them in her letter. The last version of the hymn declares:

Oh, these parting scenes will end,
Some sweet day, by and by;
We shall gather friend with friend,
Some sweet day, by and by;
There before our father's throne,
When the mists and clouds have flown,
We shall know as we are known,
Some sweet day, by and by.

That Thursday night was a typical one for Fanny Crosby—typical of her life, for that matter. She was always busy bringing comfort to others and spreading the gospel story.

After Fanny finished her letter she prepared for bed, and Florence Booth retired to her own room, not far away. Florence, however, slept lightly that night and about three o'clock in the morning, she heard footsteps in Fanny's room. She hurried to her blind aunt and helped her to bed just as she lapsed into unconsciousness. Two doctors were called and arrived within minutes, but there was nothing they could do. Fanny Crosby, just short of her ninety-fifth birthday, had gone to the land of which she loved to sing.

And I shall see Him face to face
And tell the story, Saved by Grace!

35
"Jesus Is Mine"

Newspapers published on Friday, February 12, 1915, carried the sad news around the world. Fanny Crosby had died. The *Bridgeport Post* reported, "City loses one of most distinguished residents. Though nearly 95 years old Miss Crosby was recognized as greatest writer of hymns in world—had composed more than 8,000 in addition to many cantatas."

The story further stated, "Miss Crosby's passing away was peaceful and without pain, as if she were falling into a slumber, her everlasting sleep."

Letters and cards poured in from around the globe. Before time for the funeral service to begin on the following Monday afternoon, Fanny in her casket seemed to be sleeping in a bed of flowers. Violets, the flower she had claimed as her favorite, were there in profusion. People came from many parts of the country, and the First Methodist Church was filled to capacity and overflowing.

George C. Stebbins, who had set many of her hymns to music, said of her: "Fanny wrote for the hearts of the people, and she wrote even better than she knew. She imbued all she ever did with a befitting spirit—the spirit of sweetness."

Ira Allan Sankey, Hubert P. Main, S. Trevena Jackson, and George C. Stebbins were honorary pallbearers. The choir and congregation sang "Faith of Our Fathers." The Reverend H. A. Davenport led in prayer. This was followed with the choir singing "Safe in the Arms of Jesus" and "Saved by Grace."

"You have come to pay tribute and to crown a friend," George M. Brown said. "There must have been a royal welcome when this queen of sacred song burst the bonds of death and passed into the glories of heaven."

After the services ended, Fanny's body was borne to Mountain Grove Cemetery and laid to rest. The small American flag she carried so often was buried with her.

Fanny Crosby had stated to her sister that if people wished to do anything to her memory she would prefer the money go to the Bridgeport Christian Union. This request was kept and in addition a Fanny Crosby Memorial Home was organized. This is a retirement home for Protestant Christians, and those who knew Fanny best agreed this would have pleased her greatly. It is still in operation at 1088 Fairfield Avenue, in Bridgeport.

Fanny's niece laid a small stone at the head of her grave. Only a few inches high, the stone is lettered across the top, "Aunt Fanny." The face of the stone states simply, "She hath done what she could," and below that, "Fanny J. Crosby."

That was it. Fanny Crosby would have wanted it no other way. For forty years that small stone was the only thing that marked the blind hymn writer's grave.

To many of Fanny's friends the relatively inconspicuous marker seemed inadequate. In 1955 former judge Paul Miller, trustee of the Fanny Crosby Memorial home, and the Reverend Joseph E. Pouliot, director of the Bridgeport Christian Union, decided to do something about it. They began collecting private subscriptions for a larger monument, and one was sculptured by a New York firm.

The commemoration was set for 3:30 P.M., Sunday, May 1, 1955. Services began at the Fanny Crosby Memorial Home, followed by a pilgrimage to the chapel at Mountain Grove Cemetery. Included in the program there were a number of Fanny's most loved hymns.

Officiating at the unveiling of the monument at the grave were the Reverends Joseph E. Pouliot, William H. Alderson, Herbert S. Brown, and S. Willard Samuelson, and Paul L. Miller. The group that gathered sang Fanny's hymn, "Blessed

Assurance."

The smaller marker was moved to the foot of the grave. The face of the new monument bears a thirteen-line biographical sketch plus the notation, "Erected by friends to whom her life was an inspiration." Besides these are four lines that are recognized by almost every Christian visiting the grave:

> Blessed assurance, Jesus is mine!
> Oh what a foretaste of Glory Divine!
> Heir of salvation, purchase of God,
> Born of the Spirit, washed in His blood.

36
I Knew Fanny Crosby

About forty miles north of New York City in West Chester County is a town by the name of Katonah. My parents owned a two-family house there on Valley Road. My mother's name was Effie Ruggles. The Paddock family rented one side of the house and we lived in the other.

Fanny Crosby visited the Paddock family often, and although I was a teenager and she an old lady, I remember her well. I remember she had the custom of placing her hands on the faces of those she met. That was her way of "seeing" them. The last time I saw Fanny was when I was sixteen years old in Bridgeport, Connecticut.

Although this book is written more than sixty years after Fanny Crosby's death, there are people still living who remember the famous hymn writer. The preceding statement was made by Mrs. Mabel Ferguson, who now lives in Wilson, North Carolina. As Mrs. Ferguson indicated about herself, anyone living today and remembering Fanny Crosby would have had to be rather young during Fanny's old age.

After a long, painstaking search, I was fortunate to contact and interview some of these people.

Milton W. Hobby, Sr., archivist for the Golden Hill United Methodist Church in Bridgeport, Connecticut, furnished information not available elsewhere and verified other statements. Mr. Hobby, too, remembers Fanny Crosby as an elderly Christian lady. He was young when Fanny died, but he mentioned:

You probably know that Fanny Crosby was a member of our church when it was the First Methodist Episcopal Church on Fairfield Avenue, in downtown Bridgeport. Our present designation is Golden Hill United Methodist Church and the name was adopted a few years ago, when two other Methodist parishes merged with us.

As was explained in another chapter, after the death of Fanny's father, her mother married a widower, Thomas Morris, who had three children by a previous marriage. These children, of course, were Fanny's stepbrothers and sisters. The granddaughter of one of these stepbrothers is Miss Marjorie Morris, still residing in Bridgeport. Miss Morris kindly furnished important information for this work and established as fact certain statements that otherwise would not have been included.

Although Miss Morris was a young child when Fanny died, she recalls the family Christmas parties. She remembers the little gifts Aunt Fanny made for the children and the witty Christmas cards she wrote.

"She had quite a ready wit," Miss Morris added.

Miss Morris' brother, Albert Shelton Morris, once told a reporter: "I was a young lad, and my grandaunt, slight and spent like her photographs, with her green glasses, was not a figure to impress a young lad. It was only later when I grew up that I realized how famous a writer she was."

One of Fanny Crosby's cousins was Mrs. George Weston Atwater. Mrs. Atwater's granddaughter is Cleo Atwater Crowl, who lives in Sacramento, California. Mrs. Crowl, like Mr. Morris, remembers Fanny's dark glasses and, like Mrs. Ferguson, remembers the touch of Fanny's hands on her face:

As to her physical appearance, she was quite elderly, and I was very small the only time I saw her. She impressed me as being an "old lady" and quite feeble. As I think about it now, it might have been the fact that she was treated with such love by all there, and she couldn't make a move but what some of the men were at her side to help her. I can't recall the color of her hair. I do remember she was dressed all in black, with a white ruche on a collar about her neck. She also wore a tiny black bonnet atop her head, with a bow under her chin.

The one event that I can remember vividly was at one of the family reunions. I was very young, six or seven. When Fanny arrived, I was very frightened of her because I had been told she could not see, and her black hexagon glasses made me feel very strange. I did not want to be near her, but when my mother took me over to meet her, her voice and the touch of her hand on my face had a strange affect on me. I was no longer frightened.

·My father, his brother, my grandfather, and a cousin formed a quartet for an impromptu entertainment. My father could never carry a tune, and his brother not very well. My grandfather had a fine voice, and the cousin a fair voice. You can imagine what the results were. I can remember so well them singing a round called 'Scotland's Burning!' and what they lacked in harmony they made up in enthusiasm, and Fanny laughed heartily. In fact she was still laughing after the program ended. This reunion would have been in 1907 or 1908.

Mrs. Crowl also remembers her grandmother telling her about a trip that Fanny and a companion made to Colorado. Seated in the coach, the companion described the scenery along the way. Various wild flowers bloomed in profusion along the railroad's right-of-way, and it seemed that almost every flower had yellow in it.

"God must have loved yellow," Fanny exclaimed, "for He made so much of it for His flowers!"

As has been mentioned in various chapters, almost any occasion that presented itself called for a poem from Fanny Crosby—whether it was to console someone in mourning, a birthday, a speaking engagement, or a family reunion.

Such a reunion was held in 1905, and when Fanny returned home, she sent each cousin who had been present a copy of her book, *Bells at Evening and Other Verses*, and on the cover she attached a sheet with this notation: "The following poem was suggested after a family reunion, which took place at the home of Mr. and Mrs. Fred D. Voorhees at Lansingville, N. Y., September 1905."

Mrs. Crowl graciously supplied us with a copy of this poem by Fanny Crosby, and although it was written almost three-quarters of a century ago, it is published here for the first time:

> God bless you all, my cousins dear,
> His gracious hand has brought us here,
> And through His tender love we meet
> And one by one each other greet.
>
> For this our kindred souls have prayed,
> And though the answer was delayed,
> It comes at last with smiles and flowers,
> With sunny skies and golden hours.
>
> We'll ne'er forget this glorious day,
> But live it o'er when far away,
> And oft as now in thought we'll meet
> In social converse pure and sweet.
>
> And when our eyes behold the fact
> Of Him who saves us by His grace,
> We'll thank Him for His patient care
> And praise His name forever there.
>
> Fanny Crosby

The Reverend Ernest K. Emurian, minister in the Cherrydale United Methodist Church, Arlington, Virginia, is a prolific writer. He has made extensive research and study in the field of hymnology and has himself written a number of hymns. Those who love hymns and the stories of how they were written especially appreciate his *Living Stories of Famous Hymns, Forty Stories of Famous Gospel Songs,* and his more recent *Famous Stories of Inspiring Hymns.*

Fanny Crosby died in 1915, and Mr. Emurian, of course, never knew her personally. His parents did know her and his father wrote music for some of her hymns. I had the pleasure of interviewing Ernest Emurian by telephone and letter. In a letter Mr. Emurian wrote:

> On July 11, 1909, my parents, Rev. and Mrs. S. K. Emurian were on their honeymoon, visiting the Religious Assembly Ground at Round Lake, N. Y. Mother wrote in her diary that night: "In the evening Fanny J. Crosby told how she came to write many of her favorite hymns, and stories about several of them . . . . What a wonderful woman she is. Such childlike faith, such sweet love, such cheerfulness! It put me to shame."

Mrs. Emurian devoted a number of pages in her diary to her experiences with Fanny Crosby at that meeting. She went on to tell how her grandfather, Rev. Albert Ruliffson, had founded the Bowery Mission in New York. She told how Fanny Crosby had worked with the Ruliffsons for sixteen years in that mission. Fanny Crosby, too, went into great detail about her work with the Ruliffsons in her *Memories of Eighty Years.*

In my interview with Rev. Ernest Emurian, he added: "I have cherished photographs of my parents and the remarkable blind poetess, taken that July, 1909, at Round Lake, N. Y. It was while worshiping at the Bowery Mission, while my great-grandfather was preaching, that she was inspired to write 'Rescue the Perishing.' "

In gathering material for this book, I have acquired many statements about Fanny Crosby made by various individuals, some famous and others unknown. Most of these people, like Fanny, have already passed on, but the remainder of this chapter is devoted to some of these people who knew Fanny Crosby.

In promoting one of her books, former President Cleveland said: "You who have brought cheer and comfort to so many in the past, richly deserve now the greatest amount of grateful acknowledgement, and all the rich recompense, which the love of friends and the approval of God can supply."

Foster Coates wrote in 1898: "There is no happier woman in all the world than this blind singer of God's praises . . . . Her life may be said to be one long, joyous song."

Soon after Fanny's death a drive was begun to raise funds for a Fanny Crosby Memorial Building. In a printed program promoting this drive, Fanny Crosby's sister is quoted as saying: "The last time my sister Fanny visited me she said, 'Well, when I die I don't want any big monument over my grave. If my friends want to do anything in memory of me, I would rather they would give the money for a hall down at the Bank Street Mission, to help save men.'"

And her niece with whom she lived at the time of her death said: "In the years of her life, she did what she could to bless humanity and she often said that the only words she ever wanted on any memorial to her were: 'She hath done what she could.'"

Will Carleton was a writer, poet, editor, and publisher. During the final quarter of the last century, he was popular for homespun verse, and it probably was his touching poem "Over the Hill to the Poor House" that launched him to fame. He published several volumes of poetry under such titles as *City Legends, City Ballads, Farm Festivals, Farm Legends, and Farm Ballads.* Mr. Carleton knew Fanny Crosby and wrote of her:

All over this country, and, one might say, the world, Fanny Crosby's hymns are singing themselves into the hearts and souls of the people. They have been doing this for many years, and will do so as long as our civilization lasts.

But what of Fanny Crosby the woman? Is her personality as sweet and inspiring as her poems? Has her life been an exemplification and illustration of them?

From those of us that know her well, such questions would elicit a smile. Whoever has had opportunity of witnessing her patience, her sweetness of thought and life, her bright winsomeness and her all-around and all-through goodness, would not even take the trouble to answer in the affirmative; he would say, "There she is; there is her life; let them speak for themselves."

S. Trevena Jackson quoted George M. Brown, Fanny's pastor, as saying:

By her faith, her hope and her love she more nearly exemplified the Christian graces than any other person I have ever known. Her faith was rich and full, with no taint of doubt to lessen the sweetness of her assurance. If she believed too much she lost nothing by it in this life, and certainly not in the life into which she has entered.

W. D. Stephens, a writer, made the prophetic statement that many others might have made: "Fanny Crosby died in 1915. But the record of her eager achievement and consecration will live for many a day."

While she was yet living on earth Robert Lowry, who set much of her writing to music, wrote:

Passing now through the later seventies of her useful life, she preserves all the sprightliness of her early years. Her friendships are fervent, and her hope strong. She loves her work, and she finds her rest in Christ. In her younger days she joined the Methodist Episcopal Church, and its fellowship is still her comfort and delight. She engages in no doctrinal controversies, but speaks the language of Zion with saints of every name.

On hearing of Fanny's death, the head of a Chicago mission said, "It's the sorriest news I've heard in many a day. And well do I know two men who will be sad at the tale of it." He went on to explain how two of his great Christian friends came to the Lord on hearing "Safe in the Arms of Jesus" and "Rescue the Perishing."

Annie Isabel Willis described Fanny in a newspaper story:

Miss Crosby is a small woman who talks and moves quickly. She always has a smile of greeting and a warm grasp of the hand for her friends. She is extremely happy in her chosen work, for it renders her independent, and her heart is often cheered by hearing of the good done by her hymns. She can sew and knit and perform some household duties as well, so her life is full of occupation.

Allan Sutherland wrote a story about Fanny Crosby and it appeared in the April, 1905, issue of *The Delineator*. Among his remarks were:

The work of this winsome and deeply spiritual woman has been world-wide in its uplifting influence over humanity. It is little wonder, therefore, that, as she now celebrates her eighty-fifth birthday, thousands of good men should rise up to call her blessed, and the churches unite in a service of her songs.

More than ever, as the years go by, the popularity of Fanny Crosby's hymns increases. In every gathering where the salvation of souls is the chief object of concern one or more of her compositions are sung. There are many today who can say with grateful, wholehearted sincerity, "Thank God for Fanny Crosby, and for all her labor of love and helpfulness!"

In the February, 1892, issue of *The Mentor* was a story written by Mary E. Rogers. This story concluded with these paragraphs:

Many of her hymns have stirred the hearts of listeners and awakened longing for a better life; and many a touching story of their influence is related. Her own peaceful and confident spirit breathes through her lines, and gives them power over the hearts of others.

Her industry is a marked characteristic. She is never idle. Speaking of occupations, she one day remarked that, if she could not write, she believed she would go into a restaurant and wash dishes; for she was sure she could do that well. Her hands are as active as her mind; and counterpanes and many other knitted articles are the product of her busy fingers. Her home is with a friend who has been her amanuensis for fourteen years.

Miss Crosby is a slender woman, somewhat below the average stature, with an animated and happy face, a pleasant voice, which has also a resolute sound, a trim figure, which in its neatness reminds one of the presiding genius of a New England household, and an atmosphere about her as of one whose life is occupied with the "Father's business." Her thin, worn frame shows signs of age, but not of infirmity; and now, at the age of nearly seventy-two years, this energetic woman, whose cheerful spirit sheds a sweet air of peace and happiness around her, pursues her career with undiminished vigor.

As recently as 1973 and 1974, the editors of *Christian Herald* conducted a poll to determine the most popular hymns. It must be remembered that the old hymns were not only in competition with each other but also with the modern ones which are tremendous hits for a year or two and then fade away. The results of the polls appeared in the April, 1974, issue. Fanny Crosby's "Blessed Assurance" placed eighth on the list of twenty-eight most popular hymns!

In a separate poll conducted at the Florida State Prison, her "Pass Me Not, O Gentle Saviour" was fourth on a list of five hymns. A similar study was made by a publisher in Wisconsin. On the forms returned to him, 362 hymns were named, and on the list of eleven that received the most votes, "Blessed Assurance" was number nine.

Those people who knew Fanny Crosby personally probably were in a position to know better than we what the blind lady had that enabled her to write such enduring hymns. And probably none of her friends were as close to her as Dwight L. Moody and Ira D. Sankey, the famous evangelistic team. Mr. Sankey wrote the music for many of her hymns and was instrumental in publishing hundreds of others. These hymns were introduced throughout the world in the Moody-Sankey evangelistic crusades.

It is said that during the latter part of Fanny's life Mr. Moody asked her a question, thinking he knew what the answer would be.

"If you could have just one wish granted, what would it be?" he asked, feeling sure she would wish to have her physical sight restored. Fanny apparently sensed the answer he expected and surprised him.

"If I could have one wish," she answered, "I'd wish that I might continue blind the rest of my life."

"How can you say that?" he asked.

"Because," she replied, "after being blind for all these years, the first face I want to see now is the face of Jesus!"

Bibliography

Asbury, Herbert. *All Around the Town, Alfred A. Knoph*, 1934.

Barrows, Cliff, and others. *Crusader Hymns and Hymn Stories*, Hope Publishing Company, 1966, 1967.

Bliss, P. P. and Sankey, Ira D. *Gospel Hymns and Sacred Songs*, John Church and Company and Biglow and Main, 1875.

Bradbury, William B. and others, ed. *Bright Jewels*, Biglow and Main, 1869.

_____ *Bradbury's Golden Censer*, Ivison, Phinney, Blakeman and Company, 1864.

_____ *Golden Chain*, Ivison, Phinney, Blakeman and Company, 1864.

_____ *Golden Trio*, Ivison, Phinney, Blakeman and Company, 1864.

_____ *Hymn and Tune Book*, Moore, Wilstach & Baldwin, 1865.

_____ *Hymn and Tune Book*, American Baptist Publication Society, 1864.

Booth, Mary L. *History of the City of New York*, James Miller, 1863.

Bowen, Croswell. *Great River of the Mountains: The Hudson*, Hastings House, 1941.

Brown, Henry Collins. *Brownstone Fronts and Saratoga Trunks*, E. P. Dutton & Co., 1935.

Carleton, Will. *City Legends*, Harper & Brothers, 1889.

_____ *Farm Ballads*, Harper & Brothers, 1882.

Chapple, J. N., ed. *Heart Songs, Dear to the American People*, The Chapple Pub. Co., 1909.

Crosby, Fanny J. *Memories of Eighty Years*, James H. Earle & Co., 1906.

_____ *Fanny Crosby's Life-Story*, Everywhere Publishing Co., 1903.

_____ *Bells at Evening and Other Verses*, Biglow & Main, 1897.

_____ *Monterey and Other Poems*, R. Craighead, 1851.

_____ *The Blind Girl and Other Poems*, Wiley & Putnam, 1844.

Date, Henry, ed. *Pentecostal Hymns*, Hope Publishing Co., 1902.

Deen, Edith. *Great Women of the Christian Faith*, Harper & Brothers, 1959.

Doten, Edith Kinney. *A Pageant of the Life of Fanny Crosby*, The Fanny J. Crosby Memorial, 1925.

Draper, James. *More Than a Song*, The Moody Bible Institute, Inc., 1971.

Duffield, S. A. W. *English Hymns: Their Authors and History*, Funk & Wagnalls Co., 1886.

Editors, *Christian Herald*, "Fanny Crosby at Eighty-Eight," March 18, 1908.

_____ *Christian Herald*, "The Hymns You Love Best," April, 1974.

_____ *McClure's Magazine*, "Cleveland as a Teacher in the Institution for the Blind," April, 1909.

_____ *Christian Record Talking Magazine*, "Songs of Faith," Nos. 4, 5, and 6, 1969, 1970, Christian Record Braille Foundation, Inc.

Emurian, Ernest K. *Forty Stories of Famous Gospel Songs*, Baker Book House, 1959.

_____ *Living Stories of Famous Hymns*, Baker Book House, 1955.

Frampton, Merle E. *Forgotten Children*, Porter Sargent, 1969.

General Convention, The. *The Mission Hymnal*, Biglow & Main, 1913.

Jackson, S. Trevena and Sankey, I. Allan. *An Evening of Song and Story With Fanny J. Crosby*, Biglow & Main, 1912.

Jackson, S. Trevena. *Fanny Crosby's Story of Ninety-Four Years*, Fleming H. Revell Co., 1915.

Janiver, Thomas A. *In Old New York*, Harper & Brothers, 1894.

Jenkins, Stephen. *The Story of the Bronx*, G. P. Putnam's Sons, 1912.

Johnson, Allen, ed. *Dictionary of American Biography*, Charles Scribner's Sons, 1964.

Julian, John. ed. *A Dictionary of Hymnology*, John Murray, 1908.

Kirkpatrick, W. J. and others, ed. *Grateful Praise*, Hall Mack, 1902.

_____ *Songs of Redeeming Love*, John J. Hood, 1882.

Konkel, Wilbur. *Living Hymn Stories*, Bethany Fellowship, Inc., 1971.

Lossing, Benson J. *Pictorial Field Book of the Revolution*, Harper & Brothers, 1855.

Lowry, Robert, and others, ed. *Pure Gold*, Biglow & Main, 1871.

_____ *Welcome Tidings*, Biglow & Main, 1877.

McGranahan, James, and others, ed. *Church Hymns and Gospel Songs*, Biglow & Main, 1898.

_____ *The Gospel Choir*, Biglow & Main, 1885.

McWhirter, Norris and Ross. *Guiness Book of World Records*, Bantam Books, 1976.

Moody, W. R. *The Life of Dwight L. Moody*, Morgan and Scott, 1900.

Morrison, James Dalton, ed. *Masterpieces of Religious Verse*, Harper & Brothers, 1959.

Nevins, Allan. *Grover Cleveland*, Dodd Mead & Co., 1932.

Philips and Hunt. *The Epworth Hymnal*, Cranston & Stowe, 1864.

Phillips, Philip, ed. *The Singing Pilgrim*, Carlton & Porter, 1866.

Rizk, Helen Salem. *Stories of the Christian Hymns*, Abingdon Press, 1964.

Rogers, Mary E. *The Mentor*, "Fanny Crosby," February, 1892.

Root, George F. *The Flower Queen*, Oliver Ditson Company, 1880.

Sankey, Ira D. *My Life and Story of the Gospel Hymns*, Harper & Brothers, 1907.

Sankey, Ira D. and others, ed. *Sacred Songs No. 1*, Biglow & Main, 1896.

———— *Gospel Hymns, No. 2*, Biglow & Main, 1876.

———— *Gospel Hymns, No. 3*, Biglow & Main, 1878.

———— *Gospel Hymns Combined, Nos. 1, 2, & 3*, Biglow & Main, 1879.

———— *Gospel Hymns Consolidated, 1, 2, 3, & 4*, Biglow & Main, 1866.

———— *Gospel Hymns No. 5*, Biglow & Main, 1887.

———— *Gospel Hymns No. 6*, Biglow & Main, 1891.

———— *Gospel Hymns, Nos. 1 to 6, Complete*, Biglow & Main, 1894.

———— *Christian Endeavor Hymns*, Biglow & Main, 1894.

Sankey, Ira D. Ed. *Sacred Songs and Solos*, Morgan & Scott, no date.

Sankey, I. Allan, ed. *Hallowed Hymns, New and Old*, Biglow & Main, 1909.

Shumway, Henry L. *New England Magazine*, "New England's Hymn-Writer," May, 1905.

Stebbins, George C., ed. *Northfield Hymnal*, Biglow & Main, 1904.

Sutherland, Allan. *The Delineator*, "Fanny Crosby, a Singer of Sacred Song," April, 1905.

Sweney, John R. and others, ed. *Finest of the Wheat*, R. R. McCabe & Co., 1890.

Vincent, J. H., ed. *The Epworth Hymnal*, Hunt & Eaton, 1885.

Wilson, Kenneth L. *Christian Herald*, "Compassion's Strong Right Arm," September, 1953.

Photo Credits

Photo of Fanny J. Crosby on page 106 courtesy of the New York Public Library.

Photo of Miss Crosby's friends on page 107 courtesy of the Library of Congress.

Photos of Jenny Lind, George Frederick Root, and Grover Cleveland on page 108 courtesy of the Library of Congress; photo of Mrs. Joseph F. Knapp on the same page courtesy of Metropolitan Life Insurance Company, New York. N. Y.

Photo of the Hudson River on page 109 courtesy of the Library of Congress; photo of Fanny Crosby's birthplace courtesy of Sybil Baker.

Photo of Carnegie Hall on page 110 courtesy of the Library of Congress.